155·93ł

Coping with Your Partner's Death

Geoff Billings has a background in engineering, and in occupational health and safety. He has also been a management consultant and a technical author. He lost his own wife, Ros, after a seven year battle with cancer, and was eventually inspired to write this book with the help and support of his children, Suzanne Billings and Nicholas Billings.

Overcoming Common Problems Series

Selected titles

A full list of titles is available from Sheldon Press,
36 Causton Street, London SW1P 4ST and on our website at
www.sheldonpress.co.uk

The Assertiveness Handbook
Mary Hartley

Assertiveness: Step by Step
Dr Windy Dryden and Daniel Constantinou

Body Language: What You Need to Know
David Cohen

Breaking Free
Carolyn Ainscough and Kay Toon

Calm Down
Paul Hauck

The Candida Diet Book
Karen Brody

Cataract: What You Need to Know
Mark Watts

The Chronic Fatigue Healing Diet
Christine Craggs-Hinton

The Chronic Pain Diet Book
Neville Shone

Cider Vinegar
Margaret Hills

Comfort for Depression
Janet Horwood

**Coming Off Tranquillizers and
Antidepressants**
Professor Malcolm Lader

The Complete Carer's Guide
Bridget McCall

The Confidence Book
Gordon Lamont

Confidence Works
Gladeana McMahon

Coping Successfully with Pain
Neville Shone

Coping Successfully with Panic Attacks
Shirley Trickett

Coping Successfully with Period Problems
Mary-Claire Mason

Coping Successfully with Prostate Cancer
Dr Tom Smith

Coping Successfully with Ulcerative Colitis
Peter Cartwright

Coping Successfully with Varicose Veins
Christine Craggs-Hinton

Coping Successfully with Your Hiatus Hernia
Dr Tom Smith

Coping Successfully with Your Irritable Bowel
Rosemary Nicol

Coping with Age-related Memory Loss
Dr Tom Smith

Coping with Alopecia
Dr Nigel Hunt and Dr Sue McHale

Coping with Blushing
Dr Robert Edelmann

Coping with Bowel Cancer
Dr Tom Smith

Coping with Brain Injury
Maggie Rich

Coping with Candida
Shirley Trickett

Coping with Chemotherapy
Dr Terry Priestman

Coping with Childhood Allergies
Jill Eckersley

Coping with Childhood Asthma
Jill Eckersley

Coping with Chronic Fatigue
Trudie Chalder

Coping with Coeliac Disease
Karen Brody

Coping with Compulsive Eating
Ruth Searle

**Coping with Diabetes in Childhood and
Adolescence**
Dr Philippa Kaye

Coping with Diverticulitis
Peter Cartwright

Coping with Down's Syndrome
Fiona Marshall

Overcoming Common Problems Series

Coping with Dyspraxia
Jill Eckersley

Coping with Eating Disorders and Body Image
Christine Craggs-Hinton

Coping with Family Stress
Dr Peter Cheevers

Coping with Gout
Christine Craggs-Hinton

Coping with Hearing Loss
Christine Craggs-Hinton

Coping with Heartburn and Reflux
Dr Tom Smith

Coping with Macular Degeneration
Dr Patricia Gilbert

Coping with the Menopause
Janet Horwood

Coping with a Mid-life Crisis
Derek Milne

Coping with Polycystic Ovary Syndrome
Christine Craggs-Hinton

Coping with Postnatal Depression
Sandra L. Wheatley

Coping with Radiotherapy
Dr Terry Priestman

Coping with SAD
Fiona Marshall and Peter Cheevers

Coping with Snoring and Sleep Apnoea
Jill Eckersley

Coping with a Stressed Nervous System
Dr Kenneth Hambly and Alice Muir

Coping with Strokes
Dr Tom Smith

Coping with Suicide
Maggie Helen

Coping with Tinnitus
Christine Craggs-Hinton

The Depression Diet Book
Theresa Cheung

Depression: Healing Emotional Distress
Linda Hurcombe

Depressive Illness
Dr Tim Cantopher

Eating for a Healthy Heart
Robert Povey, Jacqui Morrell and Rachel Povey

The Fertility Handbook
Dr Philippa Kaye

The Fibromyalgia Healing Diet
Christine Craggs-Hinton

Free Your Life from Fear
Jenny Hare

Getting a Good Night's Sleep
Fiona Johnston

Heal the Hurt: How to Forgive and Move On
Dr Ann Macaskill

Help Your Child Get Fit Not Fat
Jan Hurst and Sue Hubberstey

Helping Children Cope with Anxiety
Jill Eckersley

Helping Children Cope with Change and Loss
Rosemary Wells

Helping Children Cope with Grief
Rosemary Wells

How to Approach Death
Julia Tugendhat

How to Be a Healthy Weight
Philippa Pigache

How to Beat Pain
Christine Craggs-Hinton

How to Cope with Difficult People
Alan Houel and Christian Godefroy

How to Get the Best from Your Doctor
Dr Tom Smith

How to Make Life Happen
Gladeana McMahon

How to Stop Worrying
Dr Frank Tallis

How to Talk to Your Child
Penny Oates

Hysterectomy
Suzie Hayman

The IBS Healing Plan
Theresa Cheung

Is HRT Right for You?
Dr Anne MacGregor

Letting Go of Anxiety and Depression
Dr Windy Dryden

Living with Asperger Syndrome
Dr Joan Gomez

Living with Asthma
Dr Robert Youngson

Living with Autism
Fiona Marshall

Overcoming Common Problems Series

Living with Birthmarks and Blemishes
Gordon Lamont

Living with Crohn's Disease
Dr Joan Gomez

Living with Eczema
Jill Eckersley

Living with Fibromyalgia
Christine Craggs-Hinton

Living with Food Intolerance
Alex Gazzola

Living with Grief
Dr Tony Lake

Living with Heart Failure
Susan Elliot-Wright

Living with Hughes Syndrome
Triona Holden

Living with Loss and Grief
Julia Tugendhat

Living with Lupus
Philippa Pigache

Living with Osteoarthritis
Dr Patricia Gilbert

Living with Osteoporosis
Dr Joan Gomez

Living with Rheumatoid Arthritis
Philippa Pigache

Living with Schizophrenia
Dr Neel Burton and Dr Phil Davison

Living with a Seriously Ill Child
Dr Jan Aldridge

Living with Sjögren's Syndrome
Sue Dyson

Losing a Baby
Sarah Ewing

Losing a Child
Linda Hurcombe

Making Relationships Work
Alison Waines

The Multiple Sclerosis Diet Book
Tessa Buckley

Overcoming Anorexia
Professor J. Hubert Lacey, Christine Craggs-Hinton and Kate Robinson

Overcoming Anxiety
Dr Windy Dryden

Overcoming Back Pain
Dr Tom Smith

Overcoming Depression
Dr Windy Dryden and Sarah Opie

Overcoming Emotional Abuse
Susan Elliot-Wright

Overcoming Hurt
Dr Windy Dryden

Overcoming Jealousy
Dr Windy Dryden

Overcoming Loneliness and Making Friends
Márianna Csóti

Overcoming Procrastination
Dr Windy Dryden

The PMS Diet Book
Karen Evennett

The PMS Handbook
Theresa Cheung

The Self-Esteem Journal
Alison Waines

Simplify Your Life
Naomi Saunders

Stress-related Illness
Dr Tim Cantopher

Ten Steps to Positive Living
Dr Windy Dryden

Think Your Way to Happiness
Dr Windy Dryden and Jack Gordon

The Thinking Person's Guide to Happiness
Ruth Searle

The Traveller's Good Health Guide
Dr Ted Lankester

Treat Your Own Knees
Jim Johnson

Treating Arthritis Diet Book
Margaret Hills

Treating Arthritis – The Drug-Free Way
Margaret Hills

Treating Arthritis Exercise Book
Margaret Hills and Janet Horwood

Treating Arthritis – More Drug-Free Ways
Margaret Hills

Understanding Obsessions and Compulsions
Dr Frank Tallis

When Someone You Love Has Depression
Barbara Baker

Your Man's Health
Fiona Marshall

Overcoming Common Problems

Coping with Your Partner's Death

Your bereavement guide

GEOFF BILLINGS

sheldon **PRESS**

First published in Great Britain in 2008
Sheldon Press
36 Causton Street
London SW1P 4ST

The author and publisher have made every effort to ensure that the
external website and email addresses included in this book are correct and
up to date at the time of going to press. The author and publisher are not
responsible for the content, quality or continuing accessibility of the sites.

British Library Cataloguing-in-Publication Data
A catalogue record for this book is available from the British Library

ISBN 978-1-84709-051-9

1 3 5 7 9 10 8 6 4 2

Typeset by Fakenham Photosetting Ltd, Fakenham, Norfolk
Printed in Great Britain by Ashford Colour Press

Produced on paper from sustainable forests

Contents

Acknowledgements		ix
Introduction		xi
1	Initial formalities	1
2	Your new role	11
3	Money matters – personal and official	20
4	Taking charge	34
5	New skills and routines around the house	37
6	Those around you – neighbours, friends, relationships	48
7	Your security and safety	57
8	Your health and well-being	61
9	Taking stock	66
10	Your five Rs – rest, refresh, reflect, review and respond	71
Epilogue		85
Appendix 1: Have you got lists?		86
Appendix 2: Business letters		96
Useful addresses		104
Index		110

To a wonderful wife and mother, Ros Billings.
Although it came about as a result of her death,
this book has been developed to be of use and
help to all surviving partners. We hope it will
help you get through this ordeal, and beyond.

Acknowledgements

My children Nick, Suzanne and I did all we could to support each other after our loss, but we really needed and are especially grateful to all those mentioned below.

My wife Ros was extremely fortunate in spending her final days in the care of the staff and restful surroundings of the Countess Mountbatten Hospice, Southampton. We are very grateful to the staff who, day and night, were always alert and prompt in meeting the needs of their patients. We also very much appreciate the follow-up support and counselling we received.

In addition our special thanks go out to Claudine for her initial encouragement, without which this book may not have been written. Special thanks also to Father Peter, Dave and Sheila, Sue M, Ann and David (Swansea), – Dave and Liz (Canada), and 'Liz' (Asda). Elaine from the USA receives very special thanks. Their understanding and assistance always came in the right way, and at the right time, to enable us to cope with and respond to numerous situations for which we were quite unprepared; and later, too, during the healing process when we were trying to get back on track. We shall never forget their help and kindness.

Special acknowledgement

I must also include my special thanks to Nick and Suzanne for their encouragement and help in bringing all our experiences together in this book, to help those who have to face the death of a partner all alone. Without my son and daughter, this book would not have been written. They stand somewhere between being co-authors, inspiration, and staunch sources of support.

This book has been developed to be of use and help to all surviving partners. We hope it will help you get through this ordeal, and beyond. We wish you well and much better times in the future.

The author and publishers accept no responsibility for any losses or damage that result from omissions or use of the contents of this book for whatever reason, nor for the accuracy of the details of the services and organizations listed. They have been included because the author found they were able to help him and his family in their time of need. It is hoped that readers find that some of them will also be helpful to them when encountering similar problems. Feedback is welcomed on the contents of this book; the author would like to hear from readers with any comments, via Sheldon Press.

Introduction

Sadly, most readers of this book will have recently lost a loved one. That extra-special person, dearest and deeply loved, but now so very much missed. Someone who, by leaving, has left behind a huge, unexpected void in the life of the survivor.

Having chosen each other to be close companions for the journey through life, the shock is immense when one partner suddenly goes on ahead. The surviving partner suddenly discovers how much they relied on each other, more than had been appreciated or imagined. The loved one's absence brings sadness, confusion, grief, and raw emotions. This loss also means the total destruction of all the shared arrangements that used to work so well.

During the very difficult and stressful period of your life following your partner's death, you are left to face a wide variety of changes and some very difficult times alone, or with little help. You feel in need of a new companion, one that can fit into place quickly and can be trusted to be helpful – one that can remain with you while you come to terms with the situation, and can help you deal with the mountain of tasks and changes facing you both now and later; one that can also perhaps offer you support in the future when you start feeling the time is right to start rebuilding your life and world.

This is why this book has been written. By reading and understanding the approach, experiences and knowledge I gained along my journey, I hope you will find this book helpful when trying to understand and respond to the many tasks, problems, demands and situations you are sure to encounter.

My wife died after a long illness involving many ups and downs, and numerous visits to distant hospitals for treatment. Although we both had wills, and updated them from time to time, we did not dwell on the topic of death. Our wills were intended for use a long way ahead in the future, or if we became involved in a serious accident – but NOT NOW. Therefore her death came as a major shock, much greater than anything I had ever experienced. My partner in everything for nearly 40 years had gone on ahead.

Our children were young adults; both had left home and moved away several years earlier to follow their own lives. It was obvious that, being retired, I would now be living and tackling this changed situation mostly on my own. I spoke to my solicitor, and we discussed what was involved. It was suggested I should try and deal with everything myself. Looking back, I am very glad I did, because the work was extremely satisfying, both at the time, and later when I was adapting my records into a format suitable for this book. It helped to fill the big void while I was attempting to adjust to my changed situation.

Understanding this book

Coping with Your Partner's Death is not an instruction manual, or a collection of procedures to follow. This is just not possible. However, I hope that it may prove something of a companion to you as you journey through bereavement. In the past, you had a close and trusted companion with whom you could discuss things, someone who shared his or her knowledge and exchanged thoughts with you. Now, sadly, that person is no longer here and able to help you. Do not despair, because this book covers a wide variety of issues and problems that are likely to be similar to the ones you are facing, and suggests ways in which they can be tackled.

It aims to cover your needs by providing a supply of relevant thoughts, ideas, and prompts that will help you on your way. There are brief comments and experiences about the many personal matters you are likely to face and undergo. Also included are financial and legal matters relating to tax, general and probate paperwork, and acting as executor when carrying out the instructions laid out in the will.

Reference to tax issues and legal matters may start you thinking about employing a solicitor or accountant to do all or some of the work. This may, of course, be necessary for some people if their affairs are very complex. However, we live in an age with helplines and customer services supporting many activities. They are provided to assist people in situations such as this. So, if you decide to go it alone, you should be able to access plenty of support along the way. There is also much information available on the internet.

If you choose to employ a solicitor, it's worth bearing in mind that you cannot expect them to do all the work. Even professionals cannot carry out what you want them to do efficiently unless you give them adequate basic information, which you believe is reliable, from the beginning. Likewise, if they have little background knowledge of the situation, they may not always discriminate between what is and isn't important, even though *you* know. So, part of your job may be to brief professionals.

There are some initial tasks which you must do, and which will lead on to others. You will find that there are many tasks you can deal with yourself without too much trouble. If you make a start with these, and tackle the work steadily bit by bit, you are soon likely to find the overall task is very much easier than you first thought. When dealing with tax matters, remember always to obtain and comply with the current rules and regulations. If you end up puzzled in any way, most tax offices have very good helpline staff.

Each chapter of the book outlines a general approach to different subjects, which you can adopt or modify to deal with what you need to do. Even if the solutions offered may not be your way of doing things, the idea behind it all is to give you some prompts. You can think about each topic in turn and modify the suggestions in the way that you feel is right for you.

Facing your new situation

You meet that very special person in your life; you share the next ten, twenty, thirty plus happy years with him or her. Then he or she dies, leaving you not only filled with grief, but having to deal with a host of changes and unfamiliar tasks, including tax and probate.

Bereavement is a surprisingly busy time. A wide variety of things can be going on at any one time, so, while I've tried to group the various issues into relevant chapters, you may find that this is a book to dip into, rather than read through. The first chapter looks at what to consider immediately after your bereavement, and the next two look at what you'll need to think about fairly early on – say in the first six weeks to two months. The Appendices and Useful addresses section at the back will also help you to deal with the various problem areas.

The key point is that, suddenly, you are faced with a host of situations to which, probably, you have never given a thought. The terrible reality of death fights with trivia such as how to use the washing machine or work the lawnmower, and meanwhile there are serious issues calling for your attention, such as a letter from the tax office, a demand for the car tax, or the need to release funds from the bank. All jostling for your attention, while your mind is still reeling from what has happened.

In addition, now that you are perhaps living alone for the first time in years, probably still in a state of shock, you are likely to be vulnerable. Pay extra attention to your safety, and bear in mind that, not being at your strongest, you may more easily be bullied, whether it be by bank managers or by unknown callers at the door. If your partner's death means you are now living alone, think about the obvious precautions such as net curtains and blinds, timed lighting, and how accessible the back garden is. A visit from your local crime prevention officer may be a good idea.

It's impossible to take note of everything you need to think about in one go. Thoughts and issues crowd together, and in the first days and weeks you may be too numb or traumatized to really take them in. Below is a summary of the points covered in this book. Some you will know about already, others you may not yet have thought of.

Don't forget to refer to the index if you have a particular issue you want to address, such as friends and neighbours, or money matters.

- *Chapter 1: Initial formalities.* Who needs to be informed about the death; procedures to follow; the funeral; identity theft and the need for caution, even between the death and the funeral.
- *Chapter 2: Your new role.* Facing a changed world; starting to review everything; your health, and your wealth; death itself and what it means to you; beliefs and experiences; cost reduction and control – will you need to be careful with your finances now?
- *Chapter 3: Money matters.* Personal finances; dealing with organizations and professionals; starting a filing system; business letters; two months on, you're still raw but much has been achieved.

- *Chapter 4: Taking charge.* Up until now you've been able to share the load; now you're handling everything alone; organizing your own affairs.
- *Chapter 5: New skills and routines.* These may include gardening, cooking, washing, DIY.
- *Chapter 6: Those around you.* Keeping in contact with neighbours, friends; personal relationships.
- *Chapter 7: Your security and safety.* Advice if you are now living alone for the first time.
- *Chapter 8: Your health and well-being.* Do you need to take extra care now that there's no one at home to keep an eye on you?; counselling – the unlikeliest people can benefit.
- *Chapter 9: Taking stock.* A review, 9–12 months on; health; diet; holidays and visits – choosing when you're ready.
- *Chapter 10: Your five Rs: rest, refresh, reflect, review and respond.* New activities and friends; a friendly caution – separating the wolves from the sheep; how others have managed; moving on – but only when you're ready; your home – do you have to downsize?; taking stock 12–18 months on – how you may feel; will there be a happy ending?; a summary of Do's and Don'ts.
- *Appendix 1: Have you got lists?* Checklists to help you get organized.
- *Appendix 2: Business letters.* Advice on corresponding with organizations and some useful specimen letters.
- *Useful addresses.* Organizations providing help and advice, with telephone numbers and web pages.

Remember that when and how you respond to the various situations and problems facing you is always entirely your choice and decision. In several ways, this book is similar to a cookery book, as it contains different recipes and ingredients. However it is used – the ingredients, preparations, cooking, choice of meal time and ways of serving it, raw to overcooked – is entirely up to you!

While I have tried hard to ensure that the contents of this book will be useful and helpful, please bear in mind that legislation is forever changing. Therefore I can only aim to provide general help and assistance.

1

Initial formalities

Formal procedures

As you would expect after someone has died, there are formal procedures to follow. The purpose of these is to protect the interests of the person who has died. They include checks on his or her identity, and the cause of death, natural or otherwise. They also set formal arrangements in motion to ensure that the right person becomes responsible and accountable for dealing with the funeral and all other matters that arise following the death. It needs to be determined whether there is a will naming an executor; if there is no will, everything must be dealt with in a formal, lawful manner.

Your local authority may be able to provide information, advice and support about the arrangements that need to be made after a bereavement, such as registering the death and obtaining a death certificate.

Notifying authorities

First, a doctor must issue a death certificate. This is normally taken, together with other documents and information, to the local register of births, deaths and marriages. Provided that the death was due to natural causes, the registrar issues a formal death certificate, and another certificate which allows burial or cremation to take place in the weeks ahead.

You will need to notify some authorities by post. They will all want to see an original copy of the death certificate, and make their own copy. In your letters, always ask for the original certificate to be returned. Some may not deal with the matter promptly, and therefore to avoid delays it may be advisable to buy several additional copies of the death certificate from the registrar during your initial visit. This is cheaper than buying them later.

If the cause of death is uncertain and requires further investigation the coroner becomes involved, and this will mean a delay before you can proceed any further.

If there is a will

If there is a will, and cause of death was natural, you will be able to identify the executor and confirm who has the authority to arrange the funeral. If this is not you, you need to check that the named person is willing to do so. The individual(s) can decline the role if they wish. Also check what money is available to pay the costs involved. The deceased's solicitor can confirm that the will is valid and is the latest one.

Later you will need certified copies of the will, and the grant of representation, which enables the person or people named in the will to deal with the assets and belongings – or 'estate' – of the deceased. Your solicitor is able to provide you with certified copies of the will, and now is the time to request a number of these. As with the death certificate, some authorities need to be notified in writing by post and will want to see an original document, or a certified copy of the original.

If there is no will

When someone dies without a will (intestate), an Act of Parliament is applied when settling who should deal with the deceased's affairs and who should inherit the estate (property, personal possessions and money). This makes matters more complicated, especially as the regulations vary between England and Wales, Scotland and Northern Ireland. In general, in each case the order in which relatives are given the authority for decision-making is set out. This makes it extremely important for you to check, and to obtain professional guidance if necessary, to be sure that you have the authority to take on the role of executor.

In order to be able to administer someone's estate you normally need to apply to the Probate Registry for a Grant of Letters of Administration. You can ask your solicitor to help you or you can apply yourself.

The grant enables you to become the administrator of the estate, and is proof to banks, building societies and other organizations that you have authority to access and distribute funds of the deceased. Bear in mind that all bills, debts and taxes have to be settled before you can share out the deceased's remaining money, property and possessions.

For more help, you can contact the Probate and Inheritance Tax helpline on 0845 302 0900. Lines are open Monday to Friday, 9 a.m. to 5 p.m. Or visit <www.direct.gov.uk/en/RightsAndResponsibilities/ Death/Preparation/DG_10029716>.

Remember that there is a need for prompt action, and also that being an executor is quite a responsibility. The person who arranges the funeral and what follows from then on is fully accountable in all respects for everything that takes place.

Dealing with any debts

Before the estate of the deceased can be distributed according to the will, it is extremely important that an executor clears all debts and claims on an estate. If you have any doubts at all, check with your solicitor. You may need to advertise locally and in the *London Gazette* (or *Edinburgh* or *Belfast Gazette*), the official journal of records, to prevent a late claim. You do not want to be in the situation of having shared the money out, then to receive a higher priority claim needing to be settled. Should there be a complaint, probate registry can look into whether you have distributed the estate properly. It is always prudent to request a receipt when you hand anything over, even small items such as jewellery, and especially donations to the church or a charity; sometimes the named charity no longer exists, having been taken over by another organization, or changes its name, since the will was drawn up.

The funeral

As mentioned previously, the person who has the authority to carry out the role of executor needs to be identified, either from the will or by carrying out other checks. When the registrar has issued the death certificate, and the certificate allowing burial or cremation to take place, the executor can go ahead with arrangements for the funeral. The executor needs to proceed as soon as possible;

your requirements will have to fit in with other funerals already arranged.

Regular churchgoers may have already been in contact with their minister and perhaps been given some guidance on the service, and the choice of an undertaker. Others will not have had this option; but either way, however sensitive you feel at this moment, you need to start moving forward on the funeral arrangements. Painful though it can be, it is worth visiting more than one undertaker.

> ### Bob
> When Bob's wife Anne died, he and his children discussed the options with two sets of undertakers, and made their decision after due reflection: 'The first we chose from their advertisement in the local weekend newspaper. We visited their offices, and found them pleasant and helpful, but somehow the staff did not appear to be thorough in their approach when discussing things with us. The other undertaker was recommended to us by a close family friend, who in fact conducted the church service for us. This funeral director and his staff quickly put us at ease, and seemed to understand the situation and our needs and concerns. They were all patient, and explained things clearly, fully and well, even when we went back later to clarify some minor points. Everything went smoothly before, during and after the funeral.'

Appointing a funeral director

Funeral directors will give you a clear understanding of all that is involved. They are likely to be able to offer a wider range of details than you need, but you should find them willing to talk through everything without obligation. They will provide an estimate detailing the cost of everything they could provide, to enable you to finalize your requirements from start to finish.

It may be helpful for you to see a variety of service sheets that have been used in other services, some of which may well strike you as more suitable than others. Distant relatives who are unable to attend the funeral on the day can be sent a copy of the service sheet, with a copy of the eulogy.

Funerals are expensive – much more in some areas than in others. Significant savings can sometimes be made by choosing a particular crematorium, cemetery or church. Some churches are willing to accept, and provide services for, other faiths. Ministers, hospital staff and undertakers can often suggest alternatives which meet your needs, particularly if costs, location or other matters cause any difficulties. Some people may also be eligible for funeral and bereavement benefits; for a claim form, contact your local Jobcentre Plus or social security office, or you can download one at Directgov: <www.direct.gov.uk/en/MoneyTaxAndBenefits/ BenefitsTaxCreditsAndOtherSupport/Bereaved/DG_10018660>. (See Chapter 2 for more on the costs of funerals.)

Once appointed, the funeral director will explain the best way in which your wishes can be satisfied, and will perhaps suggest any minor changes that might make things go more smoothly. Funeral directors liaise with those involved at the church and/or crematorium of your choice, but you may need to have contact with the minister yourself regarding choosing the contents of the service and eulogy, or some other personal attention.

Once you have finalized the arrangements, an announcement in your local paper is the usual way of informing people about the date and time. You will probably also want or need to tell some people via telephone, letter or email. Remember, too, that there may be distant friends and relatives who should be informed. It is by no means unusual to request family flowers only, and to suggest instead that donations are made to a named charity, or hospice, by way of the funeral director.

After the funeral it is customary to thank everyone involved; an acknowledgement in your local paper will be sufficient for most, although many people appreciate a personal note of thanks; this would be an excellent way of maintaining your links with friends at this lonely time (see also Chapter 6).

Identity theft and caution

You will have heard about identity theft, and the need to ensure that your credit cards, bank statements, utility bills and the like are completely chopped up, cross-shredded or burnt when no longer required. This, of course, is to prevent misuse of the details by others.

Sadly, the need to destroy personal information in this way also applies to that of those who have died – even at this early stage of your bereavement. People who steal this sort of information have been known to create a 'person' by using the name and date of birth displayed on a headstone. In the USA credit cards have even been created in a deceased person's name and used extensively in the short time between the death and the funeral.

Therefore, please be aware that there are people about who prey on the dead in this way. There is more on this subject in Chapter 3, but, for now, bear in mind that you need to inform organizations who need to know about the death, such as banks, credit card companies, stores, authorities, as quickly as possible.

As soon as you come across a credit or store card, write down the name and number. Ring the relevant helpline, tell them what has happened and say that you intend to destroy the card immediately, together with the other related identification paperwork you have. Make a note of the time you are making this call, and also name of the person you are speaking to; instruct him or her to remove all details from their register and mailing lists. Check that this action is sufficient, in case they also need confirmation in writing. If you are dealing with a catalogue company and a refund of money is involved, the company will request a copy of the death certificate, and then will return the money to the executor.

Keep your notes of the organizations, telephone numbers, and names of the people you have spoken to in this way and the dates you contacted them in a safe place until well after the time you believe they have actioned your request. You must wait until you are satisfied that all mailing and contact has ceased, and this can take six months or more. As well as being periodic, mailshots can have been prepared six or more weeks ahead, and not all organizations respond immediately.

Do not forget that later, when you clear out these records, they too ALL need to be shredded.

If you are providing an obituary, it is suggested that you do not include precise details of either the date of birth (just the year), or your address. The latter information could be used by burglars during the funeral. It is unfortunate that this world of ours is not a very nice place at times!

Passports and driving licences are widely used for identification purposes, so it is essential that you inform both the issuing offices of your partner's death. Ask how you should dispose of the passport or licence in your possession, and if you are asked to send them for cancellation, use recorded delivery. You may be aware that the UK government is considering introducing fines as a penalty for neglecting to inform these offices promptly.

Finally, send copies of the death certificate to our nationally used credit reporting bureaus, and ask them to prevent further use in their system. Run a credit report later to check that there has been no further activity.

Notice the use of 'caution' at the start of this section. What is given here is just a little warning that you need to remember to be cautious, but not frightened. You are likely to be affected by the loss of your partner for a long time to come, and this can make you less alert, more vulnerable, and a possible target for wrongdoers.

Although most people will be pleasant, honest and helpful, the odd one may not be, and may try to take advantage of you. Be extremely cautious in money matters. Whenever you need to discuss your financial situation with an organization, always ask to speak to staff in a private room – at any time there could also be related issues which need more careful thought. Organizations such as the Citizens' Advice Bureau may offer unbiased help and advice, but banks and others are there to make money from yours. Even when you believe your affairs have been sorted out completely, and you are sure you are fully aware of your financial situation in all respects, you still need to be extremely careful at all times.

Summary: the tasks following a partner's death

In the first few days

- Your doctor writes out the death certificate. Take this to the Registry Office to register the death, and obtain the burial certificate, and extra copies of death certificate.
- Find out if there was a will and if so whether there were any special requests for the funeral (the solicitor may have a copy if you can't find one).
- Get in touch with the executor if this isn't you, so that he or she can start the process of obtaining probate.

- If there is no will, decide who will apply to sort out the deceased's affairs. This person needs to apply for letters of administration from the Probate Registry.
- Arrange the funeral by contacting funeral directors, minister, church, cemetery, crematorium, etc. as needed.
- Advise friends, relatives and neighbours about the death and funeral.
- See the solicitor, obtain certified copies of the will, and identify the executor if you don't know already.

As soon as possible

No one expects you to tackle all this at once, but, as soon as you can, you should start thinking about the following tasks. There is more detail about sorting out your finances in Chapter 3.

- Report the death to HM Revenue and Customs; obtain and start the relevant paperwork.
- Continue with probate until given grant of representation.
- See the solicitor to check that what you plan to do is correct.
- Start keeping a diary and record, noting every bit of information you are given, and all the tasks you do, such as notifying authorities. Always include details of names and telephone numbers.
- Empty a large drawer or find a good, sound cardboard box, and use the space to store all your late partner's loose financial and tax documents, statements, credit and store cards, etc. as you find them. Put all other relevant files in one place nearby, and file everything properly as soon as possible.
- Check your financial situation, noting such things as possible overpayments. Check with the bank/insurance company that funds are available for the funeral.
- Update insurance policies, such as house, contents and car, to your name.
- Check and cancel appointments, arrangements and direct debits no longer required.
- Notify employer(s), pension service/funds, banks, building societies, insurance companies, stores, etc. Start requesting details of all accounts, and financial statements on date of death; cancel

all credit and store cards in your partner's name; later, check and confirm that this has been done. Build up details needed for tax returns.

- Continue the gathering of financial information about all your partner's accounts, requesting statements needed for the annual and/or part-year tax returns until all are complete and submitted.

Documents you're likely to need

Collect the following documents belonging to your partner and keep them in a drawer or box to tackle when you can (unless, of course, you already have them neatly filed in one place).

- The will if there is one
- Birth certificate
- Marriage/civil partnership certificates
- NHS number and/or medical card
- Tax and National Insurance documents
- Pension (state and private) documents
- Benefit documents
- Copies of the death certificate
- PAYE form P60 and latest payslips if your partner was employed
- Bank, building society and savings accounts statements
- Stocks and shares documents
- Car, health, home and life insurance policies
- Mortgage statement and property deeds
- Credit card statements
- Utility and council tax bills in your partner's name
- Rental agreements/statements (private or local authority)
- Unpaid bills
- Leases, hire purchase agreements or similar (e.g. for equipment, car or furniture)
- Business documentation, such as outstanding invoices, if your partner was self-employed or owned a business
- Written/verbal evidence of other money owed to the deceased
- Property deeds or leases
- Driving licence
- Membership cards (for clubs, etc.)

- Passport
- Store cards
- Copies of the grant of representation (not available for several months); probate/letters of administration.

2

Your new role

Review your situation

After the death of a long-term partner, the survivor faces a changed world. It is not only feelings and emotions that are affected. When two people become very close, they very often fall into separate roles so that, to take a typical example, one partner handles the financial affairs, while the other looks after the house; one books the holidays while the other looks after the garden; and so on. Now, though, daily jobs and routines in and around the home, previously shared, have to be done by one person, or abandoned; and this is also compounded by the numerous formal and official tasks that accompany bereavement.

So now is the time when somehow you must find a quiet corner, sit down, and start to review things. There is no need to be alarmed, even if at first it all seems too difficult and perhaps too much for you. Take comfort from the fact that many other people, just like you, have found they were able to deal with everything, gaining strength and satisfaction from finding their way through it successfully.

Lists of the key tasks to do can be found in Appendix 1 (see page 86) at the end of this book, while the following chapters suggest ways to deal with many of the tasks and changes ahead. However, before reading on, be in no doubt that the next few weeks are going to be busy ones. Also be aware that even with care it can become a very expensive time.

But for now relax, and first briefly consider your *health*. Are you sleeping enough at night? Do you feel fit and able to do the tasks that you expect to arise? Do you have family members and friends you can call on for help? If you have any doubts, perhaps you should see your doctor now, before becoming too involved.

Next briefly consider your *wealth*. Do you have adequate funds, or is money, or rather the lack of it, going to be a problem? The section in this book on personal money matters (see Chapter 3, page 20) should be read as soon as possible; you must be aware of your financial situation before committing yourself to any costs.

Be financially aware

When you check your partner's bank balances, be alert to the fact that initially they may include overpayments by employers, pension schemes and/or benefits agencies which will need to be returned. In fact these overpayments are usually corrected by the provider so that the excess is reclaimed within the banking system. Notification of these adjustments, however, may be delayed by a week or more.

When someone dies, organizations holding funds in their name usually freeze the account and release the money only after probate has been granted. If you plan to request the early release of amounts from a frozen bank account, or expect an insurance payment to cover the cost of the funeral or meet other related costs, it is advisable that you check the release arrangements at the bank or company's head office level immediately. Ask for confirmation in writing. Never assume anything, and always check very carefully before you incur any costs.

Surprisingly, although you would think that bank staff encounter bereavement routinely, those at branch level are not always aware of what their head office will approve or reject when it comes to making payments associated with the death. My experience was that staff at branch level accepted invoices associated with the funeral, assuring me that they would be paid. However, head office thought differently and some of these costs were not paid, and later I had to find out why there was a delay in payment. The bank had decided not to pay the bill after all, but had not bothered to tell me, or to return the unpaid invoice. I had quickly to find another source of money to pay the bill.

Death and your feelings

Whatever your beliefs, hopes or expectations, birth and death are completely natural events. The first usually gives some nine months' warning and is a joyous time. The other is much less predictable, and although there may have been plenty of time for preparations, these have usually been ignored, as it is a topic normally treated as taboo.

This means that when the time comes for personal involvement, most people, young and old, are totally unprepared. There have been no rehearsals, and no warnings of the devastating shock of loss you are certain to experience. All the things that could help the survivor deal with the situation are rarely considered beforehand, and even if any were, they are likely to be incomplete.

The sad fact is that on your journey through life you have become separated from your partner. You may feel that this is only a temporary situation, and that as in other forms of travel, you have not lost them – they have just gone on ahead for a while. Whatever your beliefs, this separation makes life difficult, and can lead to much soul-searching by the survivor as to whether things should have been handled in any way differently. Were the arrangements exactly what your partner would have wished? Should we have discussed this, that and the other? And so on. As this can only happen when there is time to reflect, take comfort from the fact that you did what you thought was right at the time. No one can do better than that. There is no justification at all in reproaching yourself for anything. We can all be much wiser after an event.

Instead, try and start to come to terms with the feelings and changes you are experiencing and need to face up to. You may not have considered yourself to be a very emotional sort of person, but now you know differently. Your body is filled with grief and needs to return to normal. There is no shame in crying, and certainly, in our family's case, one of us experienced a delayed release of tears lasting a full half hour, and that was only the beginning. It is likely to take you a long time – months – before you can feel confident that you have regained control of your many mixed emotions. Even later, the wrong word at the wrong time, or a fleeting thought or memory, may well revive sadness and distress – without any warning at all. Even after four years it can still happen in our family, and we always believed we were not very emotional types of people.

The most important thing is not to try and bottle it up; your feelings need to be released for your own good. Loving someone, and being loved in return, is a moving and very powerful experience and is not forgotten overnight. If it happens to you, be thankful that you were one of the very lucky ones who have shared and enjoyed such a deep-seated and enduring love.

Death and the supernatural

You have doubtless heard about people very near to death who report seeing visions that appeared to be glimpses of an afterlife. You may or may not believe their stories, and no one can know whether the people were in fact dreaming, or under the influence of medication; but the experiences are real to them. Whatever it is that happens, people who have regular contact with the bereaved and those near death often report that it is by no means uncommon to hear that something very unusual has taken place.

I have always been a very practical sort of person. I still am fairly cynical, and used to be hard to convince that abnormal events can and do take place. However, I firmly believe that I conversed with my wife two weeks after her funeral.

I had just finished the evening meal, and had consumed no alcohol or medication. I was sitting in the lounge alone, looking through the closed patio doors towards the sunlit garden, which had a six foot high fence each side, and a thick ten foot high hedge across the bottom. Everything in sight was still, and the time was around 6.50 p.m.

I happened to voice my thoughts aloud to myself, glad that Ros was no longer in pain, and hoping that she was in a better place. To my amazement, outside on the patio, in the middle of a shrub, the end of one long branch about four feet above the ground started to answer by moving regularly up and down. This movement was the same as the way my wife had signified 'Yes' when she had lost the power of speech shortly before her death.

I continued this 'conversation', during which the branch answered 'Yes' and 'No' at the right time an answer was needed ('No' was signalled by rapid agitated movements). Throughout the ten-minute period this lasted, the rest of the garden was completely still.

When the movements outside ceased, I went out to inspect the bush and surrounding area very closely. I could see nothing that could have caused the movements.

That was not all that took place. Ros had been a keen gardener, and at the time of her funeral two tall spiky leaf palms both suddenly flowered for the first time.

The following year a baby rabbit appeared on Good Friday, Easter Sunday and Monday, never to be seen again. The year after, a new baby rabbit again appeared at Easter, but this time visited the garden over a longer period. To the best of our knowledge the nearest place with rabbits was about a mile away, and none had ever been seen in our garden during the previous 18 years!

All the above certainly took place and was not in any way caused by drugs or drink. As far as we are concerned they remain very unusual and somewhat mysterious events. We obviously like to think that Ros is in a nice place, and happy. How you choose to interpret these experiences, and anything of note that happens to you, is, of course, entirely up to you.

Essential reading

This section is intended to boost your morale just before you start off on your main job of sorting out the affairs of your partner. After reading it, I hope that you will begin your tasks reminded that so-called 'experts' are not clever all of the time, and that they and their colleagues are human, and make mistakes. So that, when you deal with them, it will be on equal terms. They will not seem so high up, or on a pedestal!

Never be overawed by banks, building societies, other financial institutions, or indeed any organization for that matter. Always remember that they employ people, and like everywhere else, some will be good, but others not so good. They also all use very big computer systems which do not always integrate properly, are subject to breakdowns, input errors, 'hacking' and software problems. It may not happen very often but it can and does happen from time to time. They are not perfect, but who is?

Hopefully, all the information you will be seeking will turn out to be correct, and be provided without problems. This is not everyone's experience so you do need to take care. Think, and keep it in front of you in letters ten feet high: it is YOUR PARTNER'S money they have been using. Banks, building societies and the like promise services and a reward (that is, interest) if money is entrusted into their care, so they in turn can make their living. So try to ensure they deal with things properly.

I am trying to knock off some of the gloss of 'officials' and 'organizations', and remind you that they will all have failings, and weaknesses of one sort or another. Don't worry if at the beginning you sometimes feel a little out of your depth at this vulnerable time. If you find something difficult to understand, ask them to repeat the explanation and make it clearer. Take a friend or an adult child with you for moral support. Or visit again later and talk to someone else, who will explain it a different way. Or go to another branch. If problems persist, say that you are considering transferring your account and general business. You never know, you may even find at a later date that it is a worthwhile move.

Janet

After Janet lost her husband Martin, her changed circumstances resulted in visits and talks with staff at nine different banks and building societies. During that time, she met and spent a fair amount of time with seven people from one organization. Out of that number, five really shone and knew their job well. Sadly two (both long-serving 'advisers' who deal with the public daily) made a number of mistakes – and sometimes had to consult their colleagues on quite routine matters.

Yet only one out of the seven warned her about some important 'small print' hidden away in the bank's terms and conditions which would have badly affected her had it gone unnoticed. So just be alert, and do not give up until you are fully satisfied with the outcome.

During those visits, Janet also became aware that speech in three 'private' areas could be overheard. She also noticed that the keyboard on a machine where the public input their PIN numbers was not shielded, and each PIN entry could be easily seen by people sitting nearby. This was formally reported, but continued to remain in service unaltered months later.

This underlines the need to take extra care of yourself and your assets at this time, taking sensible precautions without being unduly frightened. Most organizations try to monitor and respond to customer feedback, but this notoriously takes time. Janet received a four-page questionnaire asking about staff, efficiency, how she had been treated, and what could be done to bring about a quick improvement. She is still waiting for her suggestions to be taken up … and perhaps so are you!

Cost control and reduction

This book is intended to help people, rich and poor, to cope with bereavement. While some people will not have to worry about the financial side, others will need to readjust. Whatever your situation, it's not uncommon to be concerned about costs, and it can be a shock when this can happen immediately after death, with the funeral. However, it is possible to make savings, sometimes quite big ones.

> ### Bob
>
> Anne's funeral service was held in a town-centre church, and the burial took place at an out-of-town cemetery. The church hall was hired, with an outside caterer providing tea or coffee for those not attending the burial, and light refreshments served later when everyone returned from the burial. It went off well without a hitch.
>
> The funeral, hearse, car and staff charges would have been cheaper had it taken place at a small church with its own graveyard. Bob expected a number of people to attend who lived a long way away, although most of these did not. He catered for 50 people and expected those who had travelled some distance to be hungry. Although the hall seemed well filled, not much food was eaten. The caterer said that this was not unusual, so perhaps food for 25 would have been much more appropriate. Bob gave most of the leftovers away to the local night shelter for the homeless, so it was not wasted.
>
> Savings could have been made if instead he had hired a private room at a local pub or restaurant, or invited people back for sandwiches at his home (which he did afterwards anyway).

Funeral costs in the UK, which have been tracked by Oddfellows for several years, have risen in recent years, with marked regional variations, being most expensive in London. The average cost of a funeral in the UK is now (2008) just over £2,000, but it is estimated that by 2012 this will have risen to £3,350, according to Mintel Funeral Business Reports. This has led to some organizations, such as Age Concern, offering pre-paid funeral plans. When considering the costs of the funeral, it may be worth bearing the following in mind.

- Visit more than one funeral director, as costs for similar funerals may vary greatly between individual funeral parlours.
- If your partner had a pre-payment plan, it may not include everything that you would like, so you may have to pay the extra.
- Check if your partner had sufficient funds in the bank or building society to pay for the funeral. Then check that the bank or building society will release funds to pay all the expenses. Or there may be an insurance policy to cover the cost (see Chapter 3).
- The Department for Work and Pensions produces a leaflet which includes information about Social Fund funeral payments: D49 *What to do after a death in England and Wales*/D49S *What to do after a death in Scotland*.
- Ask the funeral director to give you an itemized list of costs to ensure there are no hidden or unexpected expenses.
- Only buy what you can afford – use the funeral checklist below to help you decide.

Funeral checklist

Cremation

- Hearse
- Coffin
- Funeral director's fees
- Removal
- Chapel of rest
- Family car
- Cremation fee
- Minister
- Casket

Burial

- Hearse
- Coffin
- Funeral director's fees

- Removal
- Chapel of rest
- Family car, extra car for mourners
- Burial fee
- Grave-digger
- Plot
- Minister

Later (several months, or a year or so) you may want to consider a headstone, which is paid for separately.

Free advice is available

Bear in mind that you do not have to pay for all the help and advice you may need. Citizens' Advice Bureaus and reference libraries are helpful and do not charge. You can talk to a solicitor for half an hour without paying a fee. Also, depending upon the problem, hospital staff, your doctor, bank and building society staff, and local authority personnel can all be useful sources of help. Do not be afraid to ask. They may say no, but in all probability will be able to send you off in the right direction. Your local benefits office is also another place to obtain help, as you may be eligible for funeral or bereavement benefits. Try organizations such as Age Concern, Help the Aged, Cruse and the Samaritans; there is no need for you to try and puzzle out your major problems on your own (see Useful addresses).

In my family's experience, our biggest saving came from dealing with tax and probate ourselves. With this in mind, the next chapter looks at money in more detail.

3

Money matters – personal and official

Personal money matters

Whether you are young or old, rich or poor, the death of your partner will have financial implications for you now and in the future. It is essential that you check thoroughly – indeed double-check – just what effect this has had on your finances. You must find out exactly how much money you have in the bank, and what your income will be from now on; you will need to review all your outgoings. You should also determine what steps, if any, you need to take to ensure that your account or accounts will always remain in balance, or, even better, with something left in hand. Check whether a life insurance policy has become payable, or exactly when it will pay out.

You have a little more freedom of action in finding out this information if you are the executor. Even if you are not, you must discover the state of your finances. Request statements for all current accounts as they become available. You will need these particularly covering a period of at least two months after the date of death, as salary, pension and benefits payments are often lump sums. Any excess will be reclaimed by the provider once they become aware of the situation. You will receive notification of this eventually but you must be careful in case you spend some of this money that is later reclaimed, causing an overdraft.

For tax purposes, the executor needs to know details of the balance in each of your partner's personal and joint accounts on the date that he or she died. Any outstanding debts on credit cards and the like will need to be paid. In the past, your household income may have included the earnings, pensions and money from benefits payments, or investments, of both of you. Upon death, your partner's accounts will be frozen, and some payments will possibly cease for ever. This means that you must be sure you know how much is going to be available for you to spend now and in the future. Likewise, your regular outgoings are likely to have been numerous. Are all of these still relevant and needed? Are they fixed or variable costs, and do some only appear at particular times of the year?

Probably most important of all – do you own your home outright? If not, you will have been making regular payments on a mortgage or rent and insurance. You need a roof over your head, and the cost of keeping it there can vary in all sorts of ways. Again, you need to know not only about existing costs, but also about any agreed changes in the future (and changes in the bank rate may affect these charges). Are the associated documents in joint names, and if so do they need correction? Does an insurance policy cover the outstanding amount?

Next, check the car. It may need to be re-registered in your name, and have the insurance details amended to show that you are the main or only driver. If it was your partner's personal car, you need to find out its current value as this will be required for the probate paperwork. With any luck, you will have established links with a reputable local garage, but if not, now's the time to start enquiring among friends and neighbours for recommendations.

The charges for utilities have become significant for everyone. Payment by standing order for gas, electricity, water supplies and telephone costs tends to be the norm. Take extra care and check any estimated meter readings against actual. The difference is usually in the provider's favour over a 12-month period, and often brings a rebate later. However, they sometimes get their sums wrong, so once again check your statements to be sure they are accurate. If the amount of money the provider has in hand is significant, and would help you at the moment, explain the circumstances and request an immediate adjustment and full refund.

Your local council should be notified promptly. If you are now the only occupant in the house, council tax charges can usually be reduced. If it is near year end, you may be in credit and find that there will even be something left over towards next year's charges. Finally, it is important that you find out whether any unusual or unexpected bills are in the offing, such as hire purchase charges, or an agreed late payment of purchase charges made earlier in the year. Failure to settle a delayed payment at the agreed time can incur a surcharge. Likewise, if tax has been underpaid in the past, you can expect a demand from HM Revenue and Customs. You must notify them of the death: your partner's accounts will be frozen until after probate, and you need to avoid penalty charges for any delay.

You should also contact the Bereavement Register and Deceased Preference Service to remove the deceased's name from mailing lists and databases (see Useful addresses).

The paper chase

Lead runners would set off with bags full of scraps of paper, scattering a trail for the rest to follow over moor and mountain. Time has not changed things much, except now the followers are called you and me, and the bits of paper form our family wealth!

The main challenges in sorting out someone's financial affairs do not usually require a high level of financial expertise. Those with normal levels of skills in addition, subtraction, multiplication and division will find them more than adequate. Instead you (and me) will find the work much easier if you have a reasonable memory, and some knowledge of what happened in the past, plus the attributes of curiosity, patience, persistence, and an interest in solving puzzles – particularly treasure hunts.

This may all seem rather odd, so I will explain. From childhood onwards, we are usually given at least one money box. Then we are told to save all our spare pennies in it for a rainy day, and to keep it in a safe place – all good advice, so that we start off right. It is later when things start going wrong.

When our savings grow big enough, banks, building societies, and others start showing an interest in looking after it for us. They offer high returns if we invest in this or that offer of the moment, and we accept. Unfortunately, a year or two later many of these schemes become 'oversubscribed', or fall out of favour and their interest rates start falling fast. When we notice this, it is explained that if we paid more attention we would know that they had been replaced by a new favourite, which once again offers an attractive return on the money you have available to invest, and so it continues.

We, on the other hand, like most other people, have been busy getting on with our work and life, and so we may not always notice that interest rates have fallen, except by chance. Our efforts have been directed towards finding a partner, getting married, having children, buying a house, moving home, getting better paid jobs and some fun out of life. So our time for keeping an eye on interest rates as well has been somewhat limited. When we do check, we are often surprised to find that so many other things have also changed in the high street too.

The banks, building societies and insurance companies have not been idle while the changes in our life have been taking place. Some have restructured, or changed their names due to takeovers or amalgamations, and some have even issued and shared shares. Also – surprise, surprise – new schemes for saving your money have been introduced. Many of these replace those we may have been familiar with in the past, and even more are offered as internet accounts. Other changes have included relocation of head offices, and new systems involving different paperwork and computer systems. These are more difficult to trace, but it will be worth the effort if your money could be involved.

During all the changes outlined above, of course they will have written to you, to explain what has taken place. However, there is a good chance some things will have been forgotten or overlooked, and some letters will have probably gone astray at the very least, especially if your mail has been redirected for a period. Add the fact that grandparents, other relatives, friends and neighbours also put money into money boxes, as well as perhaps lending and borrowing some. This means the true total may have become a little uncertain. The bits of paper relating to all of it may have rapidly increased in number, or become lost.

Do not forget that HM Revenue and Customs require you to keep the records of past transactions for a number of years in case they decide to investigate your affairs. This means that somewhere there should be a lot of very important paper: a large quantity of formal and official paperwork fully recording the transactions of the past and all current savings, and where they are located. On the other hand, you could be left with a real mishmash of money within the family circle, requiring a detailed search and investigation to sort it all out.

Two simple questions now are:

- Do you know where all these records are?
- If so, are you sure the records are complete and reliable?

It is obviously very important that you are able to work out how to trace everything. Your family wealth depends on it. Do not start worrying if you are unsure. Relax, look and check. Whatever you do, do not go charging off doing the first things that come to mind. It is *your money* we are talking about, so you need to plan carefully exactly how you are going to identify it all.

Hilary

When it came to sorting out the affairs of her late husband Christopher, Hilary found that the family finances were not all kept in one place. Items were mentioned in his will that did not match up with the records she found. One organization at an early stage disowned some of its own (valuable) paperwork references, and seemed unable to check or even trace how its savings activities normally take place, or how money is transferred. Although these problems took a little time to sort out, the surviving family ended up with accounts that they believed were accurate, and certainly containing more money than when they started!

This does not mean that the finances mentioned above would never have fully come to light, but only that their existence was not readily apparent when it needed to be. In this case, it became clear that a number of staff were not familiar with their own company systems, and that at least two of their main computer systems did not talk to each other very often, if at all.

The rest of this chapter concerns dealing with organizations of various kinds. You can decide whether any or all of it is of use to you. Use it, ignore it, or modify it to suit your own particular needs and circumstances. The information given cannot be appropriate for the particular problems you may encounter, but it gives an insight into the ways errors occur – and also, that the first response from a bank, building society, or insurance company may well be wrong.

So if you too are starting from an unsound base – good luck, and read on!

Official money matters

Tax

You must advise HM Revenue and Customs about the death of your partner. They will give you instructions and send you the relevant forms. In very general terms, they require all taxes due to be identified and paid, before any of the funds are distributed to others.

If tax returns are up to date, this means dealing only with the period from the start of the tax year up to the date of death. If your partner died after the start of the tax year, and had not completed a tax return for the previous year, that will be required in addition to one for the period from the start of the current tax year up to the date of death. Then the paperwork for probate has to be completed. Much later, when this has been approved and any tax identified and paid, the executor will be allowed to distribute the remainder in accordance with the will.

This may sound complicated, but once you have located all the relevant details, and been referred to their booklets, which set out their requirements quite clearly, most people find that they can complete the various forms without too much trouble. *Always* keep a copy of everything you send away.

Do not worry if at first the overall task seems daunting or difficult. Remember that helplines are available; or you can check facts online. Alternatively you can call in to your local tax office. This visit can be quite reassuring, as you may well find, as I did, that most of the staff do not know the answers either, and have to call their in-house 'expert' out from a back room to explain matters to you.

Never leave a visit or interview until you understand everything that has been said. Always take a pencil and pad with you. Write down the date, time, and names of the people you see and their answers and instructions.

Usually the people you meet this way in tax offices, banks and building societies will be patient, helpful and sympathetic to the difficult circumstances in which you find yourself. Some can be useful points of contact if you find an official, solicitor or other person is causing a delay in your response. They are aware that you have been making every effort to deal with the situation, and that some others are not always as helpful as they could be.

Solicitors

Solicitors tend to be a case in point. If they do not respond to your requests, or fail to deal with matters as they should, you can report them to the Law Society. The problem will be investigated and if the solicitor is found seriously at fault you may be compensated financially.

Bob

Several months after Anne's death, Bob's one remaining task was to get a distant solicitor to release an outstanding payment to her estate. This was hampered by the solicitor's lack of performance. After 18 months, Bob's patience came to an end and he reported him to the Law Society. This resulted in £250 compensation, though Bob was disappointed that the solicitor seemed to incur no other penalty which might encourage him to change his ways. 'I felt that in the past many others must have waited until he woke up of his own accord. Otherwise he would have been much more efficient, and not used the word "sorry" so many times in all his letters! (They were all most certainly sent as late as he possibly dared.)'

My own experiences over the years have been that some solicitors in small practices have been pompous and inefficient, although others (two practices in particular) have been exemplary. Larger firms may still include individuals who ought to do much better, but they are more likely to have specialists, and some of the latter can be excellent. The message seems to be, as in most things, be cautious until you find someone who gives you confidence that they will satisfy your needs.

Dealing with organizations and professionals

Begin by remembering that banks, building societies and insurance companies hold large numbers of accounts containing money belonging to customers with whom they have lost contact. This suggests that the person involved has either moved elsewhere or has died. Alternatively the money could have been misplaced by their staff by accident, or a change of address notification by either party could have been lost, etc. etc. Investors may sometimes forget to notify companies of address changes, or even forget about their investments, or maybe make investments without telling their partner. There are a variety of ways in which contact may be lost.

The point here is that you need to be thorough in your efforts to locate the whereabouts of all the money and wealth due to you. If you are not, it is unlikely to find its own way home.

A death in the family affects family wealth. Nobody outside the family circle is likely to have the same interest in ensuring that as much money as possible remains there. So it is very worthwhile to take an active interest in what is going on in the months ahead, preferably dealing with most if not all matters yourself.

We live in an age where computerized systems have all but replaced the personal touch. Typically when you telephone a bank, building society, tax office, solicitor or accountant and the like, a recorded voice will tell you that the call may be recorded for training purposes. This means that if for some reason you later ring up to discuss the matter further, or to complain, they can (and sometimes will) review your previous calls in order to deal with the matter thoroughly. If they claim to have no record of your conversation, and behave as though they disbelieve you, you may, as I did when I was treated in this way, be able to prove them wrong. No doubt as time progresses video recordings of meetings will become common, with or without your knowledge. They will, of course, be the ones to keep the recording.

This is unfortunate, indeed unsatisfactory, as all discussions are likely to be about money (your money), and they make their living by using your money for their benefit. Although they are basically honest, from time to time they all most certainly make mistakes. All are likely to be what you might call 'sharp', and not slow in trying to come forward with their own interests before yours.

Use your house telephone for all calls, fit an answerphone, and arrange to have itemized billing. Typically your monthly records will then detail date, time, rate, destination and telephone number, duration and cost of every call. When making calls, use a day-to-a-page diary to keep a written record of the topics discussed, with the names of the people you talked to, the outcome, and the agreed follow-up. It may seem a lot of trouble, but if you encounter any problems you are likely to find that this has been worthwhile. I am certainly better off financially through using this approach.

It is essential that you set up and use a filing system with individual sections for each organization you have to contact (see Chapter 4). In each section, file a copy of all your letters, with each reply, in date order. Do not make notes on their replies in case you have to copy them later. Instead, label and insert extra sheets in a ring binder for the notes as and when necessary and keep them all together.

If problems seem to be building up, remember that virtually all organizations have helplines to assist you. Do not get angry, keep cool – however bad the situation seems to be developing. If the person you are talking to finds it difficult to explain, or sort the matter out to your satisfaction, ask to speak to their supervisor. Persist until you understand all the facts and figures.

If a problem continues and you find it difficult to agree a settlement, they may send you details of how they propose to resolve the matter. Perhaps, if things are starting to get serious, suggest that you will next need to deal with their Ombudsman. Do not be overawed; it can still be an opening ploy. You can write to their directors, or newspaper consumer help services if you have just cause. If it is found that they have been unfair you may obtain a settlement plus compensation for the time and effort you expended. If it is warranted, just be persistent – never angry.

Reading a few of the letters sent to newspaper services shows that these organizations can and do make mistakes, and sometimes need prodding very hard if you are to obtain satisfaction.

Always keep a copy of every form you complete, everything you send, and note down everything you discuss. Time your calls to avoid lunch and finishing times, when staffing levels may be low.

Banks, building societies and insurance companies

You may expect that because banks, building societies, local authorities and other organizations deal on a regular basis with members of the public who have suffered bereavement, their staff will be fully trained to deal with the questions and situations that arise, and also have appropriate systems. Experience suggests that this is rarely the case.

First of all, collect as much information as you can at home, BUT keep it to yourself. Then ask each local branch to provide you with a complete statement, listing all the accounts and forms of savings they have for your late partner. Surprisingly, some will not find this an easy task. Similarly you may find that some of the staff you encounter at *all* levels and locations are not fully familiar with the way their company operates, or the range of accounts provided. Add to this a few computer systems which do not appear to connect with each other, and you may encounter a few problems along the way. Therefore it is worth spending some time and effort ensuring that you get complete and accurate details, which match the information you start off with.

It is probably sensible for you to deal with things yourself, as far as possible, or at least take an extremely close interest in the process. You are likely to be much more interested in your own personal financial situation than anyone else. If anything appears odd, you will probably notice it long before an intermediary might, and you can ask for clarification.

All these organizations will wish to see a copy of the death certificate, and make their own copy. Later many will also need to see a certified copy of the will to confirm that you are the executor. Requests vary as to what documents they require in order to prove your authority, and need, to acquire information from their records.

My experience was that sole accounts in the deceased's name were frozen on production of the death certificate. Joint accounts remain open, but you will need a statement covering the period up to the day your partner died, as for tax purposes half of the contents will be regarded as his or hers.

For tax purposes you also need to obtain a statement detailing the balance in all the deceased's personal accounts on the date of death.

It is also probably advisable to write to all head offices of the banks and organizations involved, to advise them of the death, and request full details of all accounts associated with them. Make no mention that you also intend to ask for these details at branch level.

Later, when you have all their information to hand, compare the account numbers and balances with the records you have at home. Do not be surprised if they do not match up, or some are missing. Always look through bank statements covering at least a full 12 months. This should show the periodic annual interest payments made on some types of savings, as well as dividends paid on shares and perhaps other payments which may help you complete your records, and perhaps tie up some loose ends. Some other types of savings surface only after a few years. If you decide to move, it is advisable to keep this in mind – remember to have your post redirected after you leave; it could be worth doing this for the maximum allowed period of two years.

Coping with muddles and mistakes

As already mentioned, discrepancies and miscommunications between branch and head offices can cause confusion and worse.

Hilary

Hilary had direct experience of how head offices and branches of the same bank may not always 'talk' to each other. When she asked the head office of her bank for account details, they in turn asked the branch to provide the information. However, Hilary later discovered that the person who gave this instruction was apparently not aware that the financial advisers working in their branches always deal with head office direct, so their records were not kept at branch level. Their helpline staff and supervisor did not know about these activities either, and were not familiar with the savings account referencing numbers used. Indeed they disowned them, although the numbers were on head office paper-work, and not used or retained at branch level!

Fortunately, the will and Hilary's own records, although incomplete, were eventually accepted as being correct. In the end, three sums of money (which represented quite a bit of money to Hilary), were traced, and added to the funds after ten weeks of correspondence and hassle. One amount had been passed on to an insurance company scheme without much supporting paperwork. Compensation was also paid, so hopefully now those errors have been corrected. But it makes you wonder what else in their systems is unreliable ...

The moral of this story is, if you think they are wrong, do not be fobbed off. Keep in contact at head office and branch levels until you are totally satisfied. Having been through several such processes myself, at the end of it all, I believe I now know more about my bank's systems and working practices than many of their staff. I have even thought of applying for a job with them!

If disputes cannot be resolved easily, they may refer to the Ombudsman, or try other ways of settling the matter. Do not get alarmed. Make it very clear what you want to know, and why; what you think the problem is, and how it could be resolved. If you find one person is difficult to deal with, ask for the name of their manager. Do not give up until you are satisfied. We dealt with six companies, and the best of these made one mistake. The worst made many mistakes, and more money was involved. Eventually it was all corrected to our complete satisfaction, plus compensation.

Keep in touch

As mentioned above, if you move home after your partner has died, and you are in any way unsure that everything has been resolved, it's a good idea to have your mail redirected to your new address for at least a year, perhaps two. Some forms of savings are tied up for periods of one, two or more years. In case you have not traced such funds during your search, this could help ensure they come to your attention when they mature, and are not lost.

Likewise, if you have any doubts in your mind, you have nothing to lose other than the cost of a stamp. Write to organizations to check whether they hold any money in your late partner's name. List all their current and past addresses. We reclaimed two small sums that had been forgotten for over 30 years!

Two months on

Two months on from the death of your partner, you should be starting to feel that you have achieved a great deal. The distress you experienced when arranging and attending the funeral is now behind you, and by now you will have made contact with a number of the people and organizations you had to inform about the death.

In many ways, this section comes as a reminder of the details and tasks we told you about at the beginning, before the funeral.

Hopefully by now you will have started to make at least some of the changes needed to your routines, and other matters around your home, in order to cope with your new situation. Now you also want to be sure you are clear about your priorities for the bigger tasks, and that you have set off on the right track.

HM Revenue and Customs work in tax years. You and they need to be satisfied that they have all the necessary details for the previous 12-month period ending on the last 5 April. Then, that they have everything they require for the current period since the last 6 April up to the date of death.

The requirements for probate go into this in greater detail, but each office will send you booklets explaining their needs with forms for you to complete. Again, if you ring a helpline, always have a notepad ready listing your questions, write down the date and time of your call, and the person's name, and note the content of their reply before going on to your next question. That way you will not get muddled up (too often). Look on it as a new job you have just started; it is quite usual for a newcomer to think about the instructions they have been given, and to go back for further guidance if they are still at all unsure.

The work you have to do is to collect the details needed to complete the forms on behalf of your late partner. The organizations holding this information are likely to include past employers, banks, building societies, insurance companies, National Savings and Investment, the pension service, and perhaps others.

However, before any of them are able to deal with you, they will need to see a copy of the death certificate, and probably a certified copy of the will. Quite rightly, they will not accept or give out information without proof of death, and without being completely sure that you have the authority to act in this way, or as the executor – in some cases, even after you have already been into their local branch and given them the identical information.

Having established yourself, you need to explain exactly what you want, or rather, what you have been asked to provide. Use the wording given on the individual tax forms, then you should get the right answer. However, sometimes you will be asked to write in for the details you require.

Summary

Reminder checklist – have you contacted these people?

- Benefits office
- Tax office
- National Insurance Contributions Office if your partner was self-employed
- Local authority
- Bank
- Building society
- Insurance companies – house contents, car, travel, medical, etc. (If the deceased was the first named on an insurance policy, make contact as early as possible to check that you are still insured.)
- Pension providers/life insurance companies
- Mortgage provider
- Hire purchase or loan companies
- Credit card providers
- Store cards
- Gas/electric/water companies if accounts were in the deceased's name
- TV/internet companies
- Any other hire/rental companies
- Royal Mail
- Bereavement Register and Deceased Preference Service to remove the deceased's name from mailing lists and databases
- UK Passport Agency
- DVLA, to return any driving licence, cancel car tax or return car registration documents/change ownership
- Clubs, trade unions, social groups, etc.
- Church/regular place of worship
- Doctor
- Dentist

4

Taking charge

Organize yourself

Partnerships usually build on each other's strengths. Only now, life has changed, and it is likely that there are many things you will be doing alone, some of which will not yet have even occurred to you.

You may have been a very tidy and well-organized couple, with a place for everything, and everything in its place. On the other hand, you may have been more like the rest of us – perhaps somewhat less organized. Either way, you are still likely to find things requiring your attention that you do not know much about, or the whereabouts of all the bits and pieces that make up the whole.

Do not panic or be overawed by thoughts of how big some of these tasks are likely to be. Be assured, if you list them in some sort of order, then tackle them steadily, you will find it is all possible. Use the Useful addresses, lists and sample letters in this book to help you work your way through the tasks (see pp. 86–104), and you will soon find it going smoothly. It may even become a useful and not unpleasant way of spending some of your time.

Dealing with things yourself, you may become more aware of what your partner did, and contributed to your partnership (often much more than you thought). It will also strengthen your confidence, and help you develop the skills and knowledge you will need when going it alone in the future.

Remember, even if you are thinking of using the services of a solicitor or other specialist for some of the work, you will still have to provide them with a certain amount of basic information. Without that they can do nothing. The more you can identify and locate yourself, the more you will be in the driving seat. Also, you will know whether things are progressing in a satisfactory manner, and therefore be in a position to ensure that your bills are going to be lower.

To make a start, are you absolutely certain that everything you need to attend to is in one place? If not, to get things under way, use a large drawer or box to store the papers and files as you collect them while doing other jobs around the house. Then, as your new filing system starts to take shape, you will know where at least some things are, and be able to transfer each item across into its correct file much more easily.

Your filing system

It's probably in your best interests to start a brand new filing system for this work. Create sets of files along the lines below, then add the records you have to hand. List the contents of each file so that you know exactly what you have at the start. Do this before you add any fresh details and information. The reason for this cautious approach is that it can be very important in the future to be able to compare all new information and correspondence with your original records.

During my own dealings with the various organizations involved, every one of them made at least one mistake. If I had not been able to compare and follow things up separately, I would most certainly have been seriously out of pocket in the short term, if not the long as well.

I was still using this level of care four years later, when I was writing a letter regarding premium bonds. I could include full references to the past. I mentioned that to the best of my knowledge all loose ends had been tidied up, then explained the changes I required. The person dealing with the transaction replied advising me that I would also be receiving £50. This should have been paid after probate two years earlier, but had somehow been missed. Had I not included the references, it would have remained undetected and forgotten for ever. In fact, nationally, there is currently around £23 million in unclaimed premium bond prizes. So much for computers, experts, and people's interest in money matters!

I suggest you set up labelled, alphabetical files, in date order (the latest of each set of documents going on top), for all the following. You can be sure that you are going to have a lot of paper in your home during the next 12 months, and this will make it easy to control:

Files for bereavement matters

One file for each of the following:

- General correspondence
- Business correspondence
- Your partner's last year's income tax and information records
- Your partner's current year income tax and information records
- Probate information and correspondence.

Files for your personal use

One for each of the following:

- Your own last year's income tax and information records
- Your own current year income tax and information records
- Your bank statements, bills for telephone (remember to have your bill itemized), gas, electricity, water, and council tax, etc.

The layout of each file needs to be the same, so you can easily compare them.

Keeping records up to date

Your aim from now on is to create and maintain records that are as accurate as, or even better than, those of the banks, building societies, and other organizations you are dealing with. It is your wealth you are protecting, so nothing must be too much trouble in setting it up, and keeping it up to date afterwards.

It will be easier for you, and quicker, if you can use a computer to produce your letters. You need to keep a record of what you do. However, if you do not use one, you can always keep your draft in the file for future reference.

When you tackle each task, keep a diary and note down what you did when. Otherwise in two or three months' time – or less – if for some reason they have failed to respond you will be unsure where the fault lies. You will probably be unlikely to remember everyone you have written to, or when, or the contents of your letter.

Likewise, if you have, and keep up to date, a simple action plan, you will find it easier and that your involvement becomes mostly actioned by others, as your records take shape.

5

New skills and routines around the house

Day-to-day tasks

Most couples share their regular tasks in day-to-day living, so you will be remarkably lucky if you know, and find it easy, to take over all the jobs you find building up. Certainly you will cope somehow, but the sooner you master them, or adapt them to suit your skills, interests and needs, the better.

In spite of the efforts to create equal opportunities in the work-place, at home some men may still be bewildered by even the basic tasks and equipment you need to master – quickly. Not to mention the many other jobs that may be waiting in the longer term! Some women do many of the domestic jobs by choice, but their late partner's jobs may have included doing the garden, cleaning the windows and putting out the rubbish. If either partner, female or male, has been going out to work and is used to coming back to a good meal cooked for them, this too is going to need major readjustment. Now it is up to you to ensure that nothing is for-gotten, and everything is up to date, and in a good state of repair.

Your regular tasks need to be reviewed even if you already possess most or all the skills needed. Many jobs may need adjusting in some way because initially one is trying to do the work of two. Reading through the following will give you an idea of some of the very basic tasks that need doing, possibly now for the first time by you, and perhaps of some short cuts too.

Of course, if your finances permit, you can always bring in outside help, and if you are living alone this can bring several ben-efits. A regular visitor not only brings some welcome company, she or he may also notice other things before you do, such as if you are becoming unwell, or if something in your home needs attention or maintenance before it becomes a hazard.

Bedmaking

Making your bed becomes very easy if you have a fitted sheet over the mattress, and another sheet under a duvet cover, and a spare pillow and pillowcase. The time taken to make the bed look presentable daily is minimal, as is the time taken to carry out the weekly bed linen wash.

Cleaning

Like other jobs, cleaning is best carried out routinely on a planned weekly basis. It is surprising that even one person living alone manages to create an amazing amount of dust, rubbish and certainly untidiness around the place (me in particular!).

Vacuuming the carpets is only part of the job. An extending 'Ken Dodd' type 'tickling stick' duster is useful for safely removing dust and the spiders' webs that can collect on walls and ceilings. These tend to appear more when the days begin to get colder, but can also be year-round.

Likewise, bathroom and cloakroom surfaces need periodic attention according to use. The kitchen especially needs regular attention, and particular care should be taken when cleaning work surfaces, and coming into contact with uncooked meat and other short-life foods.

Cooking utensils, pans, crockery, cutlery and kitchen tool attachments need to be properly washed after use. You may find that some items become surplus to requirements. Storing these out of the way, in a cupboard, will make things easier and reduce your work significantly.

Windows need cleaning from time to time, inside and out. If you don't already have a reliable window cleaner, check with your neighbours if they can recommend one they have used, preferably for a long time. Be slightly cautious: anyone who works on your windows can easily see the contents of your home, and soon gets to know your movements.

Cooking

It can often be the case that one partner has done most of the cooking, enjoying creating delights for all the family and visitors.

The shock of taking over this role can be a major one! The amount of debris, cleaning and washing up generated in the production of what may seem a relatively small meal can be astonishing.

If you are new to cooking, begin by reading the instruction books for the cooker, hob, microwave and everything else you will use. Get into the habit of staying in the kitchen while making toast and cooking meals if you are not sure of the timescales involved. Remember that microwaves (1000-watt and less) and toasters can easily set food on fire very quickly. Likewise, food left cooking too long on the hob soon ruins a nice new pan, as well as making the food taste terrible.

I have managed to limit my own burnt offerings to date (four years later) to just two meals (which I remind my children did not actually catch fire) and one saucepan. The first was thrown away after being forgotten during an unexpected, very long, but most welcome telephone conversation. The second was when I treated a chilled meal as if it was frozen.

Initially, and indeed in the longer term, you can enjoy very tasty and varied meals that only need heating up if you buy packaged, pre-cooked meals at supermarkets. Adding fresh vegetables is easy, as even these can be purchased prepared and ready for cooking, in small mixed packs. A wide range of prepared desserts is also on offer, along with yoghurts, and assorted fresh fruit portions. Most of these are obtainable in single portion sizes, so it is well worth checking what is on offer.

When, perhaps at a later stage, you become more adventurous, it may be worthwhile buying a small swing lid grill (these are slightly bigger than a toasted sandwich maker) on which you can cook fresh and frozen meat, etc. evenly in just a few minutes. Their best feature is their non-stick surfaces which can be cleaned quickly and easily after use.

Ironing

Whether you are a beginner or not, you may think that ironing is time-consuming and to be avoided whenever possible. But you must keep up appearances, particularly if you go out to work.

Regarding the skills required by a beginner there are two: read the instruction leaflet for the iron so you know how to use it properly, and always check that the heat setting matches the fabric label on every item you iron. If you are uncertain, place a damp cloth over the item, and lower the heat setting. Only increase the heat if the iron is having little effect on the material. This may seem over-cautious, but it is the safest way until you know what you are doing. My standard approach is to always start off with the lowest heat setting that might work.

A personal extra hint: renew trouser creases and the like well before they have disappeared, so you know where the real edge should be.

One of my first adventures after a long absence from ironing was to try and attach an 'iron-on' pocket, which came without fitting instructions. The first attempt resulted in the new white pocket instantly disappearing. Being nylon, and the iron too hot, it had dissolved into a black paste that spread over and became very securely attached to the face of the iron, securely blocking all the steam vents. I eventually managed to rectify the situation by rubbing the nylon coating off onto an old, very rough piece of towelling, and later slowly clearing the vents by discharging steam through them from two fills of water.

My next attempt to secure an 'iron-on' pocket appeared to be successful, but it fell off two days later. By then I had had enough and took the trousers to a specialist sewing shop for repair. I now tackle only routine ironing!

Sewing

This isn't likely to be a major task for most people, apart from replacing the odd button, or making good the occasional hem or seam, jobs that are not too difficult. When you have the opportunity, it is worthwhile locating shops that stock needles and thread, and finding a sewing service that carries out more complicated repairs and makes up curtains. When this sort of information is needed, good neighbours can be worth their weight in gold.

Shopping

If you use a computer, creating a standard shopping list for every trip to the supermarket, with space for extras, is a good idea. It will save time if you list items so they match the layout of the store. Use the list to check your needs and keep wastage low as well. If you get to know the staff on your regular visits there, so much the better. As I mention elsewhere in this book, you can easily become lonely when living alone. So every opportunity spent widening your circle of friends and contacts is time well spent.

You may find that clothes shopping has now become more difficult. You used to be able to rely on someone to tell you whether a proposed purchase suited and fitted you properly. Now, unless you are willing to ask the views of nearby shoppers in your age group (and perhaps making new friends), you will have to make your own judgements, or rely on your trusted friends and neighbours being honest enough to tell you what they think of your purchases.

Personal hygiene

Washing and bathing as normal is, of course, a must. Do try to make this a priority, as you need to look after yourself even if you don't feel like it; even on those low days, a shower or bath can lift your spirits a little.

Washing and drying

If using your washing machine is a new experience, once again, take time to read the instruction book. There are three main concerns.

- *Use the right amount of detergent.* Too much detergent will not rinse out properly; too little, and the clothes don't get clean. Some larger packs of washing powder provide a cup to help you measure, so try to buy one of these to get you going even if afterwards you prefer to stick to different size packet. Powdered detergent can tend to stay in lumps in the drawer. Liquid detergents or pre-measured tablets are alternatives. You can also buy laundry balls into which you put the correct amount of detergent to place in with the washing.
- *Select the correct temperature.* Be sure you select the correct temperature for the fabrics you are washing. Overheated clothes can shrink and become unwearable.
- *Note fabric colours.* Items washed at the same time should be of similar colours: keep whites and pale colours, bright colours, and dark colours separate. That way any loss of dye during the

washing process will have little effect on other items in the same load, and will keep you looking smart for much longer.

The drum capacity of your washing machine limits the contents of each wash – try not to overload the machine. This should encourage you to establish a weekly routine so that you know for sure you are up to date with keeping things clean. Consider washing all towels on one regular day, doing sheets, pillowcases and night clothes on another, and washing clothing in batches as and when needed in between.

Socks are worth a special mention. Each sock seems to have a mind of its own. Like buses, you have none at all until suddenly three or more appear at the same time. Try using a net laundry bag to keep them all together in the wash.

Using fabric conditioner can be helpful in reducing the need for ironing. However, it tends to reduce the absorbency of your towels. There are many products for all sorts of stain removal, and also for things like limescale reduction. Depending on local water supplies and your activities it is up to you whether you think their regular use is worthwhile; alternatively have a small stock in case of an unexpected emergency.

Your ability to dry washing outside in the fresh air is obviously affected by your location and the weather. If you use a tumble dryer, again cautions apply regarding excessive heat. High heat level applied to some fabrics can cause shrinkage and other damage. You can give a fresh smell to your washing by adding lightly perfumed tumble dryer sheets. You must remember to clean all filters regularly.

Gardening

Not everyone likes gardening but, if you have a garden, it needs to be kept tidy. You can let some of the more infrequent jobs slide for a while, but give some thought to ways to make the tasks easier. Grassing over or putting down slabs can reduce maintenance, while heavy pruning can help reduce the amount of cuttings and leaves you have to deal with in the future. It may be worth getting a professional in for larger or more complicated tasks.

Specialists may also be required to tackle big jobs, such as tree-trimming. A good one will work much quicker than you, using the right tools and taking away the debris afterwards. Neighbours or your local trading standards officer may be able to recommend reputable local firms, so you know that their estimates and work will be reliable.

Never give such work to people who come uninvited to your door asking for work or distributing leaflets. Most only give a mobile phone number so you have no idea whether they are local or not. Nor can you check whether they can be recommended by other people who have been satisfied with their work.

DIY, maintenance and servicing things

Even if you are totally inexperienced in home maintenance, small jobs in and around the home can often be resolved by a visit to a DIY superstore, or other larger warehouse type store. They often provide leaflets describing routine tasks, and also usually employ one or two ex-tradesmen, and older people with a lifetime of experience in carrying out small plumbing, carpentry, gardening jobs and the like. These capable people may well be able to spend a few minutes with you explaining things and giving advice, so that you know the best, cheapest, and safest way of resolving your problems.

Books with easy-to-read and understandable instructions are also readily available.

In particular, you need to know from the start whether the job involved is likely to be within your capabilities, or whether that would be too dangerous and it requires a professional. Replacing the fuse in a plug for an appliance, for instance, could probably be managed by most people – if you know that is what is needed, you have the right tool, and if you have some spares of the same type and rating – but your gas central heating boiler should only be serviced by a registered tradesperson.

It is worth assessing your possible needs well before jobs require urgent attention or you have an emergency, and compiling a list of recommended local firms. That way you will be prepared and able to turn to someone who is known to do a good job. Once again, neighbours and friends, as well as your local trading standards department, are often able to recommend suitable people.

Twice a year

Remember that the settings on all timers and clocks around the house need changing when the clocks go back and forward one hour, and some will also need adjusting if there is a power cut. So you need to know where they all are and how to do this. Unless they are already kept together, collect all the instruction leaflets together, and start keeping them all in one place.

My experience

After the funeral, some friends invited me to stay for a while. However, by then I had already started dealing with the essential tasks, and did not want to break off and perhaps forget some things. I decided that if I was going to be living alone for the foreseeable future, the sooner I got used to it the better.

I dealt with everything in the ways described in this book, breaking off as and when required to learn how to cook again, and do enough of the domestic tasks to get by. Our home help fortunately continued to come in briefly to keep things clean, and make sure I did not disappear under a pile of dust. Watching her helped give me some ideas, and I started dealing with some of the clutter we had accumulated around our home. I realized – somewhat belatedly – that a home is a type of museum which it takes two to keep in order. When there is only one to do this work, it can soon start to look a mess. The bits and pieces forming your original surroundings can begin to take over very quickly if you are not careful.

There were a few things that upset me every time I saw them. So I moved them out of sight, just putting them away in a cupboard. Then later, when I was sure there would be no regrets, I disposed of them.

I began to notice that I was surrounded by a number of dead plants. Originally they had always looked very nice around our home. It had never been my job, so I had not thought about the need to water them. I removed them all, then later, as suggested by my daughter, from time to time I bought a bunch of flowers to put in a vase to brighten up my lounge. This was all part of my way of learning about the problems, then establishing new routines, and bringing about the many changes that I gradually introduced over the next few years and will continue with in the future.

When it was fine and I had a free hour or two, I made a start on tidying up the garden. Due to our circumstances, this had been neglected for several years, so there was a lot to catch up on. My way was not to deal with it by sorting out one area at a time, then moving on. This would have created a big contrast between the cared-for and neglected areas. Instead, I stood back and looked around to find what really needed attention. Then I did enough of what was needed to tone it in with the rest. I repeated this approach over the next few months and slowly it started to take shape and look nice again.

I used the same approach to catch up on maintenance jobs indoors and outside. I was still beavering away with the bereavement paperwork most of the time, but I also needed some fresh air. The exercise made me tired so I started to sleep better too.

My days started to take shape. I am a morning person, and normally wake up early. So I would make a cup of tea, and listen to the radio for a little while before getting dressed, then take a quick walk to our convenience store to purchase a paper, and perhaps a few oddments. Usually this meant I also saw and spoke to one or more of my neighbours. Then breakfast, and about this time the post arrived and was read. After this, my efforts to deal with the paperwork commenced as soon as I had got it all in order.

Telephone calls I dealt with differently. You get to know when waiting times on helplines are longest! So I rarely called first thing in the morning, at lunchtime, or late afternoon. Also, you can waste a lot of time and money if you ring up, join the queue, talk, and then ring off, only to remember that you have only done half the job. I usually tried to make my calls mid-morning or mid-afternoon, after I had prepared a few notes about everything I wanted to say, and all I wanted to find out.

My weekly supermarket food shopping expedition was always carried out early morning, as soon after waking up as possible (I hate queues – and shopping itself for that matter). I soon got to know one checkout lady quite well. It was usually fairly quiet, so we would have a quick chat, and as we became friendly she came to learn about my circumstances. What happened then was amazing.

It became clear that she remembered most, if not all, of the many items I purchased from week to week. She started reminding me when I had either forgotten something, or was doubling up on purchases. Similarly if I purchased something new, she made sure I knew how to cook it, and regularly offered helpful comments. Her memory, and interest in my welfare, certainly helped to ease my way back into domestic matters. Even now, she still helps in ensuring I keep to a healthy and balanced diet, as well as brightening up my time spent on this chore in her store.

Our family came to know many of the staff and volunteers at the hospice, before and after my wife's death. One helper was also a bereavement counsellor who attended my church. Fortunately for me, she agreed to call in and see me from time to time. Her visits every four or five weeks helped a great deal in getting me to adapt to my new situation, and start to move forward. The hospice support group also invited me to a series of short evening meetings. Some of these involved half a dozen or so people who had been bereaved about three months, plus others with a further three months' experience. We discussed the problems we were having, and how we thought we were coping. All found it difficult at the beginning, but later we agreed we were benefiting from these exchanges of experiences and confidences.

While this was going on I completed the various tax returns paperwork, and collected all the information needed to apply for probate. When this had been sent off, I decided I deserved a treat and would visit some of the friends who had invited me. Luckily my counsellor warned me that I was still in a very vulnerable and emotional state. She suggested that, out of two suggested visits, I should consider which one was likely to be the most relaxing and peaceful, rather than stressful. I took her advice, and sure enough the visit was peaceful, quiet and undemanding – truly excellent and it did me a lot of good.

This made me put off the other visit I had planned for another month. Even then I was unprepared for what I encountered. The arrangements made were all well-meaning, but quite unsuitable for me at that early stage of recovery. Sadly I was very glad to return to the isolation of my home. It was at least another six months before I started to feel I could cope with that particular stressful environment – a great shame because they were and still are very good friends of mine. Unfortunately even people who have known you a long time do not always appreciate that you are likely to suffer from emotional problems for a long time after your partner's death. Or that recovery from your loss must be at your speed and in your own way, not what is thought suitable by them.

By this time the grant of representation had been given and I was able to carry out the requirements of the will. This was after I had discussed the matter with my solicitor, as it later became necessary to introduce a deed of variation within the permitted timescale.

With my tasks now completed I was then able to plan how I could proceed further down the road to recovery. I was coming out into the light again, and starting to leave the dark black tunnel behind me, even if there was still quite a way to go.

6

Those around you – neighbours, friends, relationships

Neighbours are important

Much has been written recently in the press about people no longer being very neighbourly. Certainly there have been major changes in people's lives over the last 50 years or so, seemingly not all for the better. Current government policies prevent, or make it much more difficult to hold some previously enjoyable social activities. Rules and regulations require a fee to be paid in order to have a street party or parade, people have to be checked before they are allowed to teach other adults, or to mix and take leading roles in social groups such as church, scouts and guides activities. However, some of these changes do not seem to have done a lot of good. The money the authorities concerned expected has not been raised, or, so it would appear from press reports, the weaker members in our society have not been protected in the intended fashion. Certain regulations have, however, well and truly destroyed some enjoyable community activities for the majority, and weakened relationships at all levels.

Moving on from this, everyone likes to be able to say that they have nice neighbours. Some are even described as being so nice, you would hardly even know they were there. It is something people like to hear, and certainly helps when selling and buying your home, and contributes to enjoyable living! However, the reverse side of this is that when you experience a serious illness or bereavement, you no longer want this remoteness; instead, a little bit of interest, contact and help would not come amiss, particularly if you are elderly, or living alone.

Bob

In Bob's situation, his experience was that, yes, his neighbours did know that he had various serious problems during his wife Anne's long illness. And yes, when he needed an emergency major operation because he too had cancer, there were two offers to assist in accompanying his wife on some of her visits to London for treatment, and with shopping. For this they were truly grateful because they were nearing the end of their tether. Apart from the above, however, which was certainly a big and welcome gesture in keeping them both alive, most of their other neighbours kept their distance. Maybe they did not want to pry, or much more likely, they were so busy dealing with their own lives they did not feel they had any spare time to help. Or perhaps they did not feel able to take on what might be seen as an apparently open-ended commitment. Fortunately, two personal friends, who lived in the area, managed to fill the gaps. So Anne's treatment and Bob's own recovery continued uninterrupted, until he was once again able to take over these tasks.

Philip

During the six months after his wife's death, Philip was invited round to friends for a few cups of tea and coffee, and one evening meal. Another invitation was talked about but never materialized. That is all, apart from the efforts of two elderly ladies. They began to make it their business to keep a watchful eye on his welfare. In the past he had given them a hand with their household emergencies, so now it was their turn. They helped him in domestic matters, such as the purchase of net curtains. They were also caring: 'You shouldn't be going up ladders at your age,' and the like. They sprang into action very much later when they thought romance was in the air, making it their business to surreptitiously vet and finally approve the lady who re-entered his life (an old friend).

He compared their response with that which happens in small-town USA. There a regular meal may be brought round, and direct offers of help made. However, even this level of help is overshadowed by the normal behaviour of residents of US retirement villages. Apparently everyone makes it their business to keep a close eye on each other. When illness or bereavement strikes the 'casserole brigade' goes into action and during the period it takes for the unfortunate person to adapt into their new situation they are regularly supported as needed. Personally Philip thought the latter approach could be (subject to age) a little over the top, but at least it is all well meant, and freely offered.

If adequate help is offered and given, you are very lucky, but if on the other hand you are left to fend on your own, you have no option but to ask your neighbours when things get desperate. Then if all else fails call on your church, social services, or perhaps a local branch of charities such as Cruse or the Samaritans for guidance and support. Whatever you decide to do, if you are in real need of help, do not delay long before asking someone.

Changes in personal relationships

The death of your partner affects every facet of your life. This includes one very important aspect of your future well-being – your relationship with your family, relatives, friends and neighbours. Sadly, you need to be aware, and accept from the start, that the relationships you enjoyed in the past may well change in unexpected ways in both the short and longer term. You are going to discover as never before that people react in very different ways, and can be completely unpredictable.

Everyone I spoke to who has lost their partner has been surprised by the behaviour of some people they thought they knew very well. No doubt this sounds a little worrying, but it is better that you are aware of such possibilities earlier rather than later. It will enable you to make allowances, and avoid being as upset as you might otherwise be if you had been taken by surprise. You will be less puzzled, and will not blame yourself for what may happen; you will also be less likely to worry that you have done something wrong and caused the situation, or outcome.

Two big changes have taken place (and no doubt many smaller ones) which will affect your relationship with others: the death of your partner, and the resulting fact that you are no longer part of a couple, but regarded as a single person.

In the first few months of your loss, your own emotions will be very raw and sensitive. Therefore you need to be aware that any changes you experience in the behaviour of others towards you are not directed at you personally. Sadly, they appear to be common to all those who are bereaved. Other people may be embarrassed, or find it difficult to accept death as an unwelcome but natural event, which perhaps questions their own life term. Take comfort from the fact that there will be others who show true understanding and friendship, and some of these will be new people entering your life, who will help fill the gaps.

We are all different, and you are unlikely to find out exactly what any individual person is thinking or feeling. There will be as many reasons for different behaviours as there are people. However, the sorts of reactions you may experience from relatives and friends are likely to be similar to any of the following:

- Some may avoid attending the funeral, no doubt because they are very upset, but perhaps because they feel threatened by death too.
- Others do not express sympathy in any way, and start to treat you as though you have always lived alone.
- Some people will talk around the person who has died and somehow avoid all references to death, regret or sympathy.
- Others, when walking towards you, will see you, then cross over the road to avoid having to speak to you. Perhaps they do not know what to say.

Fortunately, these incidents will be balanced by other people coming up to you specially; perhaps they don't know what to say, but don't want to pass by without speaking to express their regret and sympathy. In one case, I was able to repay this type of support from a lady nearly four years later when I met her again just after she had lost her partner. This time I most certainly knew what to say.

Some people do not wish to say or do anything which you might find hurtful, and so avoid talking about memories from the past and the like. Many find the new situation difficult to handle, are embarrassed, and perhaps worried how you will respond.

Most people are totally unaware how deeply one is affected by the death of a partner. Everyone will have their own personal thoughts, which obviously vary from person to person, on how long you will, or should be, affected by your loss, without ever having experienced the situation themselves. Many seem to think three or four weeks is about right!

Your loss has brought death close to them perhaps for the first time. They now realize that they too are vulnerable; they have become frightened and somehow want it all to go away. Because they cannot face their reaction to the situation, they try and ignore it. Or they may have their own interpretation of what you are feeling, and why, and consider that handling things their way will help to heal your wounds.

Likewise, because you are now single, some may look on you as a challenge to their own partnership, and seek to keep you at a distance; while others may feel that a single person no longer fits into the make-up of the group. This can sometimes result in what you might feel is odd or inappropriate behaviour.

Michael

After Michael's wife Laura died, two of her childhood friends did not attend the funeral or make any sort of contact at the time. Instead, seven months later at Christmas they sent a card with a note inviting Michael to call in when passing! Several other people also totally ignored Laura's death and funeral, and what the loss meant to the entire family. They then wrote months later expressing sympathy. One person even wrote as though Michael's wife had never existed.

Bob

One of Anne's close friends, who had known them both for a very long time, including their children and hers, rang and asked to visit Anne's grave. As this was before the headstone had been installed, she was not sure about the location. Bob arranged to meet her so he could show her where it was. On the day, she arrived with another friend, someone else who had known Bob and Anne socially. Neither of these friends wanted to talk to Bob, only to follow his car to the cemetery. They mentioned that they had lost several other friends during the previous six months. They left some flowers, before driving off and disappearing out of Bob's life for good.

Sadly, other people who have lost their partner say that these experiences are by no means unique. You may find that those who act in these unexpected ways include far too many friends of long standing whom you thought you knew very well. It is easy to be offended and upset by such actions, but remember that there will always be some people trying in some way to keep in touch.

Letters can be another source of upset and misunderstanding, especially as you are probably more sensitive now than ever before. It can be difficult to appreciate that if someone has written to you when they are upset, they may not have read through their letter to check for possible misunderstandings before posting it. But just think: would they have taken the trouble to write at all unless they had some interest and affection for you and your welfare? Surely not – so give them a second chance.

The loneliness and sadness you will experience after the death of your partner is unpleasant. If you find it at all helpful to maintain contact with friends whose actions have upset you in some small way, ignore the hurt for the time being and give your friendship a second chance. Keep in touch, even if at times they seem possibly uncaring. You are not at your best either right now. Wait until you are sure the worst is over and you feel yourself again. When the choice is yours, only then decide what you want to do, so you do not make a mistake you will regret later.

It may take a lot of effort to keep in contact with your friends, but it will be worth it because you will need help from time to time. Show them you are grateful and appreciative when they do things for you, and show you kindness. Build up a small stock of cards – thank you, get well, sympathy and birthday (mark up your calendar in advance) – plus stamps, so you are never short. This way you will always be prompt in showing your interest in maintaining the relationships still around you.

My children's experience

Suzanne and Nick

We had both flown the nest before our mother became ill. She never complained, and made a tremendous effort to live a normal life. Seven years later, after many ups and downs, the fact that we were all unprepared for her death showed how very successful and brave she had been.

Just like everyone else who experiences the death of a loved one, we were all shocked to our very roots by grief, with deep feelings of loss and great sorrow. The impact was much greater than anything we had ever experienced. This was in spite of the distraction of having jobs to go to, bringing daily contact with sympathetic friends and colleagues.

It was obviously much worse for our father. Having retired, he was now alone, and facing the need to revise everything that had developed over the years to meet the needs and happiness of our family, and then just two people. In addition there was the need to deal with all the new tasks brought about by bereavement – the funeral, plus the associated legal, tax, financial and related matters, and the changes in relationships.

At the beginning we were able to help a little. Then, he quickly decided to tackle the remainder himself. Later we all realized that keeping occupied was a much better way in helping him come to terms with things. Fortunately he had worked in large organizations as both trouble-shooter and consultant. This helped a great deal as he encountered several unexpected problems, although our finances were neither complicated nor major. Indeed we imagine our circumstances were very similar to most other families. However, incorrect information and delays were encountered because staff (at all levels), in a variety of organizations were not familiar with their own office systems and procedures, or in dealing with the outcome of bereavement.

Our father overcame these problems by working steadily in a careful and tidy manner, always double-checking results and answers, and bringing probate and the associated affairs to a successful conclusion.

Afterwards we reviewed all that had taken place, and been achieved. We realized that his notes and records formed a sound framework which if developed and expanded could be helpful to others with less experience facing similar challenges. This included his later efforts to overcome what had become a lonely environment. There was a need to find new activities and friends in order to rebuild his life. His efforts and feedback were quickly shared, and were assisting others long before this book was completed. In fact, that is how we came together to produce this book.

Six months on

Looking back over the last six months, there hasn't been much fun, has there? Your partner's death, the funeral, working out new routines, and having to tackle a lot of difficult tasks for the first time – all have made for a rather hard few months. However, you have achieved a lot, and are starting to come to terms with your new situation. Life does go on, and things can and do improve if you try and help them on their way. You have been filled with grief, sad and worried about the many tasks facing you, and are certainly not the happy person you used to be. Hopefully, now you are starting to feel a little bit better, and perhaps even sleeping more regularly than you were. So well done.

When you think about it, there must have been other times in your life when things went wrong, and looked really black too. Then a rainbow came into view, and the world seemed a much nicer place, didn't it? Well, now perhaps it is coming to the time when you are going to be able to relax a little as well. So make sure you are ready to take full advantage of every opportunity.

You've probably experienced a time in the past when you put your hand into your pocket and found there was nothing there. A time when there should have been enough coins to pay for your newspaper or bus fare. Exploring further you found a small hole, and then that the money was there, still safe, but deep inside the coat lining. Your problem now is to get the money back out again so you can pay without a huge queue building up behind you. Oh dear! Well, now is the time to start looking for your next silver lining.

In your current situation you have probably been spending a lot of time on your own, and have had few reasons to be happy. There has been no one around to tell you how well you have been doing all the tasks, or to remind you when you deserved a treat. So start thinking about the progress you have made, and give yourself a pat on the back. Look at yourself in a mirror and smile, then, trying even harder, look again. You are now on the start of an upward trend. Having passed through much of a dark tunnel, you are nearer to being out in the sunshine again.

You haven't had much to smile about at all, and most people will be unaware just how difficult you have been finding life. You need and deserve some recognition and encouragement. Any sooner, and it would have been when you were still swamped with other priorities. Any later, and you will be less inclined to react because you will be more settled in your ways. You are probably still tackling the remaining tasks, but beginning to have a little bit of spare time. So it is very important that you make use of this spare time to make a start now. It is an essential ingredient for your future happiness.

Yes, at the beginning it is going to be quite difficult for you to pick out very many things that make you happy, and give you satisfaction. However, they *are* out there if you only take the trouble to spend some time thinking about them. Get to know what they are. Start by recognizing that your glass is not half empty any more, that instead it is always half full. We are all watching and waiting to see you start smiling again!!

7

Your security and safety

Security

Our newspapers always seem to be full of reports of burglaries, wilful damage, intruders and the like. Although the overall situation could obviously be better, it is not usually as bad as it might at first appear. You need not be frightened, but it is sensible to take a few reasonable precautions so that you do not encourage unwelcome attention.

Always keep your front and back doors and gates locked, with the keys nearby for your use only. If you have any doors open at the back during hot weather, always close and lock them before going to answer a caller at your front door. Have a peephole in your front door through which to vet callers, and a safety chain in place, before you open the door.

When people live alone, it can be more obvious when their home is unoccupied. Therefore giving a little care and attention to this aspect is time well spent. Go outside and look at your house front, back and sides in the daytime, and again in the evening when it is dark and the indoor lights are on as normal. Does it look well cared for from all sides, or neglected, empty or occupied? Can passers-by easily see into any of the rooms, or when there is uncollected mail below the letter box? Do you need some additional indoor or outside lighting, perhaps some with movement detectors? Do you always leave your car parked in the same place? Would it be better to park it in your garage, if you have one, when it is not in use? Would a 'Beware of the Dog' sign on your side gate be a deterrent? Do you and your neighbours have burglar alarms, or are you the only one who does not have one?

Ask your local crime prevention officer to come to check that your doors and windows, locks, bolts, viewer and door chains meet modern standards, and are in good condition. This will provide comfort and reassurance if all is well, or useful guidance and suggestions if additional precautions are needed when you go out, or are away from home for any length of time. You may also want to consider other additions to suit your surroundings.

If you don't already have them, plain net curtains for windows, and perhaps vertical blinds for patio doors are not very expensive, and both quickly provide more privacy, and security. Likewise, the regular use of timers for a few table and standard lamps can help your home appear occupied when you are out and about. Fit energy-saving bulbs to ensure your electricity bill is not affected by doing this.

Finally, how do you deal with strangers who come to your home? Use your viewer or peephole if you have one, and keep the chain on the door until you are sure you know who they are – even if they have an identity card. If they give you a telephone number so that their identity can be confirmed, never ring that number; always look it up yourself to check, whatever clothes they are wearing. Visits by gas, electricity and water company employees are usually only made to read meters; they never come to inspect installations without prior notice. If there is more than one person, STOP and think why, and ask a neighbour to come round and assist you if you are at all unsure.

A common ploy is for a stranger to say that there are problems with the water, electricity or gas supply, and that they need to enter your home to check it. What you need to remember is that you alone are responsible for these services within your home, after the supply meter. Therefore if there is a problem, it is you and not them who needs to call for the supplier, or an electrician or plumber to sort things out.

A sensible precaution is to have a card in your telephone book with the numbers of your local authority, police, gas, electricity, water and telephone services already listed. You may also consider having a personal alarm, hanging behind the door, ready to be used just in case.

No genuine caller will be offended if you refuse to admit them until you have confirmed that they are genuine. Likewise, do not give admittance to children or adults you do not know who say their ball or pet is in your back garden. Tell them you will go and look yourself. Then close and lock the door again before you go and check.

Safety

Living alone means that you have no one around either to help you or to get help if you are suddenly taken ill, slip, trip or fall and injure yourself. Likewise, although it is to be hoped that this won't happen, if you were involved in an accident away from home and became unconscious, how would you be identified? How would hospital staff know whom to contact, or what medication you need or are allergic to?

Therefore, on a personal note there is further action to take. First of all, look in your wallet or handbag and ensure that what you carry with you always contains your name, and the names and telephone numbers of those who should be contacted if you became ill or were involved in an accident (but don't give *your* address). It would be helpful to doctors if this also included details of any medication you use, and any other relevant medical information, including your doctor's name, address and telephone number. Pendants and bracelets are available, which look quite pleasant and have a hidden compartment in which such details can be kept. These precautions are not looking on the black side, but self-preservation.

If you don't have a mobile phone, seriously consider starting to use one, and having it with you at all times (including at your bedside). Check that all the important names and numbers are stored on your phone, and the battery is fully charged. (Several names and numbers were still missing when I checked mine the second time after a minor emergency.)

Alternatively, or perhaps as well, invest in an alarm necklace or bracelet which automatically calls for help for you in the event of a fall. If you are undertaking tasks with an element of risk, such as going up into the loft, or working in the garage or a part of the back garden which isn't overlooked, remember that you are out of sight, and certainly out of neighbours' minds as well, unless you have told them what you are doing.

Remember that if you hurt yourself there are parts of your body you cannot see and you will need assistance to find out the extent of the injuries.

Now more than before, you need to make sure that your surroundings don't present hazards: check that floor coverings are in good condition, secure and not slippery, and with nothing likely to trip you up. Also make sure your house is well lit, and that handrails on flights of stairs and along landings are firm and secure – and that you hold on to them when going up and down stairs. Get in the habit of always switching a light on if you get up in the night for any reason, so you can see where you are going. If you find the brightness stops you going back to sleep quickly on your return, use a very low wattage bulb, or have a small torch to hand instead. Never wander around in the dark when you are half asleep (or wide awake for that matter!).

When cooking, never overfill pots and pans so that the contents can overflow, either to scald you or to make the floor slippery. Regularly check that pan handles are firm and secure. If pouring hot liquids into another container, always use one that both has a stable base and cannot shatter from the shock of the sudden heat. Have you got smoke and carbon monoxide alarms, and do you regularly check them to ensure that they are in good working order?

Don't leave items on the stairs (tempting perhaps if you are clearing out) as they can become a tripping hazard.

Inside and outside your home, when using ladders or step-stools be particularly careful. Outside, check that your paving slabs are level. Take extra care when mowing the lawn, and using hedge trimmers or other sharp tools with a high risk factor. Always wear appropriate clothing and footwear, as well as the recommended safety goggles, etc. And STOP before you get tired.

At home have on your noticeboard a list of emergency phone numbers. Also pin up the names and telephone numbers of relatives, close friends and neighbours, your doctor and surgery, your solicitor, church and minister – any information that could be helpful to you or others in an emergency.

8

Your health and well-being

Health

Good health is very precious, and over the first few months of bereavement you will experience a lot of stress and changes, so you need to devote extra care and attention to your well-being both now and in the long term.

This is particularly the case if your partner did all the cooking! Not only have you to relearn rusty skills, but do everything else too. Good regular meals are a must, plus frequent checks on your weight. It is all too easy to start comfort eating, or drinking all the wrong things; conversely, some people find that they forget to eat, or feel it's not worth making a meal just for one, and so may lose more weight than is desirable. Good diet is particularly important as you are likely to find that you are not sleeping very well either. After a partner's death, it is by no means unusual for normal sleep patterns to be disturbed for several months, or that for a while you can manage on much less sleep than usual.

The sooner you can identify and establish routines that suit you, the better. A regular diet plus a sensible amount of exercise, hopefully accompanied by some visits from one or two kind and trusted friends, will help you to appreciate that the world is not bad all the time. Remember too, among all the chaos and changes you are experiencing, to maintain contact with your doctor and dentist as and when needed.

The recovery period from your loss will be entirely personal to you. It may be quick, or very slow, or anywhere in between. It should always be the way you personally feel about things, and what is right for you. Changes should never be rushed or forced, or imposed on you by someone else to speed up the process or slow it down, but should depend on you, provided you have thought things through carefully. There should not be a problem with this, unless you have become depressed, in which case you must seek help from your doctor immediately. Signs of depression can vary, and aren't always distinguishable from grief, but may include loss of interest in normal activities, feeling tired all the time, sleep problems, poor appetite, irritability, finding it harder than usual to make decisions, and feeling useless or guilty. Do consult your doctor if you feel you're not recovering.

It is very easy to fall into the trap of thinking that you are coping well, that everything is fine, and that you do not need to do anything more to improve your well-being. This may well be more noticeable to others, as Suzanne and Nick found.

Suzanne and Nick

For quite a long time – several months in fact – we were both very worried about our father. He was coping with all the tasks, but seemed quite unable to be his normal self even for a brief moment or two. It came as a complete shock to him when we eventually mentioned it, at a time when a situation arose where he should have relaxed, and found time to laugh again.

You may, like me, have been brought up to keep a stiff upper lip, and not readily show your emotions. However, whether you do it in private, or in the company of others, you will find yourself experiencing uncontrollable periods of crying. There is nothing wrong with crying – it helps release some of the grief bottled up inside you, and for the present it is an essential part of your well-being. Indeed, even when you think you have things under control, for some time (probably well into the future) you are likely to find that a word, thought or unexpected event will catch you in a raw sort of way that brings your tears flooding down. You will not be able to help it, so do not try and fight it or be ashamed. Just be very grateful that you had such a wonderful partner, and loved each other so much.

As you are alone, your mental state must not be forgotten either. There are so many unexpected things happening that you have to deal with on your own. If you find that things are getting on top of you, or that life is becoming extremely difficult, do not hesitate to seek help. There will be someone out there who will find ways to ease the pressures you are experiencing. (See Useful addresses at the back of this book for details of organizations that can provide help.)

A few other suggestions to help you along the way:

- Pay attention to food hygiene (see the section on diet in Chapter 9). Weigh yourself regularly.
- Locate your medical card.
- If you take tablets on a regular basis (and who doesn't these days) start using a day/time pill-box so that you know where you are with them.
- Use a calendar and diary to ensure that you do not forget doctor/dentist/hospital appointments.
- Remember to have your annual flu jab, if you qualify for this, and have regular health checks, plus hearing and eyesight checks when needed.
- Keep a small stock of medical items so that they are readily available when needed: plasters, medicines and eyewash, etc.

Finally, always remember that life should not be all chores. When you have completed a task that has been worrying you, give yourself a treat. A bunch of flowers brightens up the darkest room.

Counselling and aftercare

Before it all happened, you were probably one of the many who find it difficult to understand why any bereaved person needs counselling or longer-term support beyond the first two or three weeks. No doubt now you have changed that view, and are wondering what is the best way of satisfying your needs. Sadly, you are likely to find that your friends and neighbours expect you to make a quick recovery without much help – unless they too have suffered a similar loss. The reality of the experience, as you now know, is somewhat different from what others often expect.

Your little world is in turmoil. You have suffered a brutal shock. You are alone for perhaps the first time in years. You have no one to confide in. You are undergoing an unwanted and enforced major new experience. Periodic, arm's length support from someone who is aware of and familiar with the problems, situations and experiences you are facing can help you keep on course.

Not everyone lives in an area where such support is available. If that is the case, I hope this book will help, as it describes the emotions and situations you are likely to encounter, and reassures you that however difficult or unpleasant your problems may be, they can be overcome. If counselling is offered, you have little to lose in giving it a try. Anything that might help reduce your level of upsets and concerns is certain to be of benefit to you.

Not everyone feels a need for counselling, or welcomes the idea of support from total strangers. Some people are perhaps a little frightened, or embarrassed, by the thought of what they imagine to be involved. They may envisage it as perhaps yet another new and difficult situation to be faced and overcome.

As someone who is normally a loner, to my surprise I found counselling very helpful, and would suggest that it is worth at least giving it a try (my children found it helpful too). However, if you feel that you do not relate easily with the person or people offering support, don't give up; enquire whether there is someone else you can meet. As with all professions, there will be some practitioners who understand and relate to your needs, and others who are poles apart. Indeed you may find, as I did, that the best of all the 'experts' I encountered, the person who was able to smooth the way for me via a number of brief visits, was a volunteer, and not a full-time professional. She continues to be a highly valued and trusted family friend.

Another form of help and support can be through contact with others who have suffered a similar loss with a timescale close to your own. Even if it appears to be a daunting prospect, a careful and controlled sharing of problems, feelings and emotions can be reassuring and comforting. Not only does this help spread the load, it can provide some prompts about things requiring attention now and in the future, knowing how others are finding ways of tackling them.

Some people do not find attending self-help groups very easy, and not all who start persevere with it. However, experience suggests that those who do continue feel that they gain a great deal from the experience. So, be gentle with yourself: don't force yourself to go, but every so often give it another try, perhaps for a bit longer this time. Think in terms of months rather than weeks.

Even 12 months later, properly led groups can still provide comfort, and can assist people along the road to recovery by helping them share their feelings and experiences. Having experienced a loss similar to your own, group members have a better understanding of what you are going through than anyone else, and can share their ways of dealing with the various situations you are all encountering.

9

Taking stock

Stand back and reflect

Some months after the death of their partner – this varies, but it may be from around nine to 12 months – most people feel able to carry out a sort of stock check about themselves following that difficult period: what they have achieved, where they have got to in all the changes, and how they wish to continue in the future.

Over the recent months most, if not all, of the things you have had to do probably presented themselves as a series of crises that you dealt with to the best of your ability. The tasks that the two of you used to do you have tackled yourself, as you became aware of them, perhaps in a fragmented, unplanned way, coping with matters such as tax and the car as and when they came up – fire-fighting, if you like. You have dealt with all these problems by taking on new tasks, developing new skills, and making a lot of changes in your daily life. You have probably had little time to think, being aware only of the need to respond to the issue of the moment, without considering the consequences in longer term. Never mind: you have coped with it all, and kept your head above water, so very well done. When these kinds of problems come your way now, you even relax a little. You know that whatever the world throws at you, you can deal with it. You have been there before, done it, and have a cupboard full of T-shirts to prove it. Well, now's the time to stand back, when things have eased up, and reflect on what you've done, and how you'd like to continue.

Taking stock doesn't mean moving on – yet. At this stage you are probably not ready to do so. You are still making the gradual and painful transition from living as one of a partnership, to sailing your own boat again. But this review of the immediate past will help you sort out where you are, what commitments you have, which ones you may need to drop, and – not least important – where you stand with general health and well-being. You cannot move on until you have sorted out the past. Part of this may be making conscious changes in the way you've been approaching life. Perhaps you've been trying to keep up the house and garden exactly as they were while your partner was alive. This is natural. Now, however, maybe it's time to let go of some of these jobs. This can be sad in some ways – it may represent yet another goodbye to the person who was so much part of your life for so long.

However, now is the time to give yourself some priority. For example, if you don't like gardening, why not pave part of the garden over, or get a gardener in once or twice a month? There is no point spending time struggling to keep up with uncongenial tasks. Once you've got things straight and have eliminated tasks you don't want to tackle, you will have time to spend on what you do feel drawn to, such as a painting class or hiking or whatever.

Therefore this review has no boundaries. It is all too easy to settle in a comfortable rut, and let the world go by. This book wants you to come out of the woodwork and start to enjoy life again, to get ready to put in that little bit of effort that would enable you to have a better time, and bring you to life again.

Whatever plans are taking shape, you should visit your doctor and dentist, so that you start off right on the health front. It does not matter whether you are young or old, rich or poor, fit or disabled. You see, in order for it to be meaningful, this review should cover health, diet and the way you have adapted to this new situation. So put a complete day aside for yourself, and start as soon as you wake up in the morning. Begin to compile a list of points requiring attention.

Health

Look at the clock. Check that you had around seven or eight hours' sleep last night. Consider whether your sleep pattern is fully back to normal. If it is, that's great, but if it is not, try and work out why. Start your list with any health concerns that you need to talk to your doctor about.

Next, get on your scales and check your weight. Is it what you think it should be? Have you been comfort eating, or skipping some meals? Add weight to your list, if it is a concern, and also to ask your doctor if you need to have your blood pressure and cholesterol levels checked. When a friend of mine, Ben, found that he was getting overweight and his cholesterol level was a little too high, he corrected it in under six months by changing his diet only very slightly (see below).

Now look in the mirror. Do you see someone nice smiling back at you? If not, what can you do to change this image? It is easy if all that is needed is a visit to your dentist or the hairdresser, a facial, or some nice clothes. If, however, it is your social life that is suffering, then for the moment do nothing more than add this to your list.

Diet

You have been very busy during the past year or so, and may not have given your stock of food the attention it deserves. Check the 'best before' dates of all the food in your cupboards, and in the freezer. Even if you are careful, supermarkets do make mistakes – it is easily done if you are in a rush – or you may, very naturally, not have noticed that some food has gone past its sell-by date.

Then check the contents of your refrigerator. Like anyone else, you should try to have a regular healthy diet. Try to eat plenty of salads, fresh vegetables and fruit, stick to low-fat spreads and desserts, fish and lean meat. Having a bottle of wine or cans of beer in the fridge is OK as long as they stay there. When they come out, they should, of course, be consumed only within the approved levels.

When Ben needed to lose weight (one stone) he was very surprised to achieve the required loss in six months without additional exercise. He did it just by cutting all fat off the meat he ate – chops, cutlets, cooked ham, pork and beef slices – and by removing the skin from barbecued chickens; he also ate less cheese and changed to soya milk for his tea and coffee. After six months he went back to semi-skimmed milk and has had no further weight problems since, apart from the after-effects of meals out or Christmas and birthday celebrations, which need a little more care!

Jobs around the house

You have probably taken on a lot of additional jobs, both indoors and out. Think about them all in turn. If you like things the way they are, great; if not, see what you can do to make your life more enjoyable. If they have not worked out the way you expected, now is the time to make some further changes. You are the one who has to be happy in your surroundings, and if you can reduce your workload in any way at all, so you have more free time, so much the better.

Friends and neighbours

You will be extremely lucky if you do not have to add to your list of points that need attention the fact that you are lonely. Fortunately, other sections in this book will help you deal with the various ways you can tackle this problem.

Holidays

Even after several months, any plans to go away on holiday may still be a long way in the future. For many, they could stay there for quite a while. Going away alone seems rather daunting and better put off until tomorrow. So let's give the idea an airing, and spend some time identifying the problems, and see how they could be overcome if and when you feel the time is right for you.

Well, it cannot be time or distance. These days the world has become much smaller. European destinations are just an hour or two away, and planes are very reliable these days. It is not unusual to fly across the Atlantic for a weekend, sightseeing or shopping in New York. Indeed some people fly all the way to Australia just to watch a cricket match. So time and distance are unlikely to be a problem – unless perhaps you use our railway network during holiday seasons.

Should you have concerns about your destination, the country and place you are visiting? Well, no; through holiday programmes on the television, books, magazines and the internet, everyone can be well informed about what to expect wherever they decide to go, or what they choose to do on arrival. Other programmes cover the work of airline staff and couriers at distant holiday resorts. So you know that help would be on hand. So where does that leave us?

Slowly we are starting to face up to the fact that for the last umpteen years you have always gone away together, perhaps with your children as well. To go it alone seems very different, difficult, and challenging. Perhaps it is in some ways, so what can be done to smooth your way?

A first step might be a short visit to friends. Perhaps when your loved one died, you may have had offers of sympathy and help, plus an invitation to stay. This may have been declined at the time – for many people, it is just too soon. At the time it was declined, but in the not too distant future might come the right time to follow it up, particularly if your friends are easy-going and you expect your surroundings will be peaceful. A few days in a new place with fresh company can work wonders for your health and confidence, even if initially, like you, people find it a little awkward, this being the first time your partner is not there too.

Later, when you know that going away to friends is bearable, why not break your journey on the way back? Try an overnight stay and day somewhere you have always wanted to visit but have never been. However difficult you imagine this could be, surely you can put up with everything you are likely to encounter during just one day? At the end of that day you will have satisfied a long-term wish, and gained some knowledge of what, if anything, you need to do to make your next away day even more enjoyable.

Your confidence can be built up in this way until you reach the stage where you can consider the idea of a holiday abroad. Now we have some good news for you. You are not alone in facing this situation, so there are a number of organizations and holiday companies that arrange holidays especially for people who can be regarded as 'singles' like yourself. They are not aimed at matchmaking, and reputable firms will have reliable arrangements in place to protect the welfare of those travelling.

10

Your five Rs – rest, refresh, reflect, review and respond

Decision time

By now, possibly around 18 months have passed since the death of your partner. This is about the time when many people can start to think about their future in a reliable sort of way. A time to consider what you have achieved, where you are, where you seem to be going, and much more important, where you really would like to be heading.

At this stage you may find that you are beginning to review your options and wishes for the future, and maybe even starting to leave the past behind – not in the sense of forgetting it, because we know that's impossible, but maybe finding yourself in a position where your lifestyle has thinned down and you now have gaps in your time to fill in. I can't emphasize enough that this can't be rushed, and in some senses may never be finalized. As a cynical person who used to take on disputes with trade unions, and win, there are still times, four years later, when memories of the past bring tears to my eyes. The same happens to a lady I know who lost her husband nine years ago. But it does mean moving on from the initial state of bereavement, where you're in shock and perhaps too emotionally unstable to consider the future with any clarity, to a time when you may be wondering if there is any chance of a happy ending.

In previous sections I have included the odd prompt regarding the possible need to make some new friends, or take up new activities. This book is for anyone who has suffered bereavement and readers will range from the young to the very old and anywhere in between, and come from a variety of backgrounds and surroundings.

Young or old, you have gone through a major crisis in your life. Well, now these pressures are off, and surely it is the time to look at your five Rs: rest, refresh, reflect, review, and respond to where you are now. Start to move over towards living more and more the way you would choose, especially if that is much different from what has been imposed on you.

Consider all the changes that have happened. Have they worked out as expected? Do you need to do anything to make improvements? Are you satisfied with your current situation? What seems to be going right, and what seems to be wrong? What do you want to do with your life? Have you thought about your long-term future, and if so, does it all seem to be working out as you would wish?

Do you need to make a fresh start of some sort? Are you lonely and in need of more friends? Are you bored and looking for a new hobby? Most important of all, are you happy? Look in the mirror and check that the person there is clean, alert, well-presented and smiling back at you. If it is a sad, unhappy face, the sooner you do something about it the better. Look back at Chapter 9 where we discuss health, and maybe think again whether you need, for example, to do something about your general health, weight, exercise, blood pressure, cholesterol, food, or medication to put things right?

Moving on

Some people who have lost a partner remarry within six months; others, long after their bereavement, are still living in a home completely unchanged from when their partner died. The home has become a shrine. They have no reason, and see no need, to move forward. Providing they are not totally isolated, this is not necessarily harmful, although this lack of progress in moving on could affect their relationships with others.

Living in the past means that the present and future are blocked out, so newcomers can feel unwelcome. One way to understand this is to divide your life into clear compartments, such as:

- What you have done, and what you have achieved
- Your childhood
- Your teens
- Your early adult years

- When you first met your partner
- Your life together
- Children
- Other landmarks such as job promotions, house moves, special holidays, and so on.

These are all parts of your life that you will never forget.

Now you are at yet another crossroads, and have to plan what to do next. This obviously needs to be what is right for you, but if you have children it will be very helpful if you have their support as well. Do not be put off by your age, illnesses, or other possible handicaps. Try and find a way to work around them, so that you can identify and achieve some new goals.

You could develop new skills, travel to exotic places, use a skill to make and sell things, learn a trade or start your own business. There are many, many opportunities out there, just waiting for you to come along and take advantage of them. In today's paper there was a photograph and article about an 88-year-old man seeking a new partner, and another item showed a pretty young woman who had given up her career as a model in order to train to be a bricklayer.

So what are you waiting for? What are your goals going to be? Just bear in mind that you never know what's round the corner ...

Philip

Philip was quietly putting his life back together after his wife's death, but before long he was distracted by the attentions of two ladies who took him under their wing. Then he came into contact with a female companion of his from the past – someone he had known for 50 years. She had recently lost her partner. Until then, he had thought that being over 60 meant that he was well past his sell-by date. Now he knows differently – so you never know.

Just look out for the bright side, and you will always find ways to bring some happiness back into your life, and others' lives too.

Your home – downsizing

You are likely to get over the shock you have suffered and complete your tasks more easily if you remain in familiar surroundings. You have more than enough to do and think about in the immediate aftermath, so given the choice you do not really want to add to your problems by also moving home, unless you have no choice.

It is ideal to delay such a big change for at least a couple of years. Wait until the time comes when you begin to think clearly about what you want to do in the future. Only then – if you still feel you need a change – will you have the time to begin to check things out properly. A move is expensive, and something you cannot afford to get wrong. If you are considering moving somewhere new, be sure to try it first by means of a short break or holiday. Stay in the area for a while, and see what it is like at different times of the year.

Never move in a hurry. Some people move to Devon or Cornwall, or to Spain and beyond after brief summer holidays there. Only when they actually start living there full time do they discover that the summer season is short, or that it is a quite different place during the rest of the year. It may be windy, too hot or too cold, too crowded or deserted, medical facilities may not be adequate: not the heaven they expected.

If you plan going further afield, prepare a list of points to check when you visit. Talk to estate agents, but remember that they will concentrate on the good news because they want you to buy. Read the local papers, and talk to the locals if you can, and find out any problems that are causing them concern. Is the local economy shrinking or growing? What is the cost of living like? If it is a small town, is there a bigger one nearby with the facilities you need, and if so is it easy to get to?

What is important to you? Look around and think about what is available. Is there an airport; a railway station; a bus service; a good hospital; a civic centre; more than one bank (bear in mind that local branches may sometimes close down); building societies; garages (for petrol, car purchase, repairs and hire); dentists; doctors and surgeries; post offices; newspaper shops; solicitors; estate agents; builders; supermarkets; shopping malls (for furniture, clothes, etc.); restaurants; cafés; garden centres; local markets; pubs; schools; colleges; churches – and so on.

Are all services available and reliable – gas, electricity, water, refuse collection, postal service, taxis, emergency services.

Does the area ever suffer from flooding, heatwaves, other disasters?

There are other things to think about when downsizing including the unexpected.

Philip

Initially, Philip found his temporary move into smaller accommodation ideal: room sizes just right, lovely surroundings, peace and quiet, nice pub meals nearby; indeed nearly everything he had expected, including being able to dispose of some furniture and house contents.

However, he soon began to put on weight. He had not realized that, because his flat was smaller than his old house, he did not get as much exercise moving around his home as before. No stairs to go up and down, less walking in and between rooms, no lawns to cut or flower beds to weed, less to decorate, and so on. He had to really cut back on food until he worked out some new activities and routines to compensate, before he got himself back in shape again.

New activities and friends

There is an old saying, 'Beauty is in the eye of the beholder', which is, of course, very true. You see couples of all shapes, sizes and looks. Some will seem attractive (to you), others less so, yet they have all found someone to accompany them. You can only guess at the depth of their relationships, but most appear content with life in their own way. So where does this observation leave you?

Did I hear you say, 'I wish I could ..?' Well, what is stopping you? Now could be the time you are thinking about taking up a new hobby or activity, or finding new friends. So why not follow it up through to completion?

Unless you are exceedingly fortunate you will surely benefit from adding new activities and people to your life. Many people experience a few voids in their life after they have completed the many tasks you have faced during the recent months.

This could be an excellent opportunity to try activities you may have only ever thought about in the past, and never got around to doing. Your local library will have lists of colleges and local social groups, as will your village hall, community centre, local newsletter, etc. Remember, however, that you have lived a fairly sheltered life during the past 12 months. Don't start off with anything too boisterous. Take it nice and steady at the beginning until you feel confident, then widen the variety. On the other hand, try not to be a sad, shy, retiring wallflower. Two of the most friendly and cheerful people I have ever met have both had ongoing problems throughout their lives – serious accidents, illnesses, family deaths – yet they never show it in public. They somehow always seem cheerful, so make sure that you make the effort too.

Adult colleges offer all sorts of classes: watercolour and oil painting, archaeology, photography, computers for beginners, the internet, or academic subject study classes. Any of these could make good starters. As might sewing, cooking, and gardening subjects, if you have a leaning (or need!) in that direction. Alternatively if you feel like something more energetic try swimming, keep fit classes or, if you live in suitable locations, horse-riding, sailing or rambling. Other groups might include birdwatching, or going out wining and dining from time to time.

If you are not in full-time or part-time work at this point, you could consider paid employment of some kind. Or you might want to make a change in the work you do. A new job need not be too demanding, unless you want it to be. Receptionist work at an optician or a dental surgery would keep you occupied and meeting people all day long. There would always be people to chat to. The advantage of this type of contact is that it is natural, in normally safe surroundings and conditions.

At some time in the future you may decide that you would like to venture into making more personal contacts, in one-to-one meetings. There are a number of ways to do this, but you need to be careful. Remember at all times that although strangers may seem pleasant on the surface, there will be one or two underneath who are not. You need to be sure before lowering your guard. A voice on the end of a phone, especially a mobile, can be anyone, anywhere, wherever they claim to be living.

Ways to meet people on a one-to-one basis include newspaper advertisements, agencies and, of course, the internet. Be aware that you have no way of knowing the motives of the advertiser. Anyone can place any sort of advertisement, and it could be serious, or it ⌐   ⌐ a joke, to see what they get in the way of replies. No one ⌐rily who they say they are, or can seem to be.

Agencies will make checks of one sort or another, but they cannot be 100 per cent correct in their assessments. Their business is the introduction of apparently compatible people to one another. Security is not their main priority, but they usually suggest that some caution is needed. All make it clear that they accept no responsibility for the outcome of their introductions. Some of the people you meet will be genuine. You just need to take your time to find out and be sure.

If you decide to explore these or similar ways of meeting people, read the section below on friendly caution. Also read carefully the advice and warning documents provided by the service, employer or agency you use.

Peter, Maree, Jack

What love, affection and the effects of habits mean to one person can mean quite different things to another. In the same way, the healing process can vary tremendously: well under six months for some, perhaps nearer to three years for many, and much longer for others. No criticism of this is justified, however short or long the period. It must be what each person chooses to do, without outside pressure from anyone. The point is that the bereaved person will never forget their late partner or that period of their life, but – although only at what they consider to be the right time – they may well feel the need to choose fresh ways and respond to new situations.

You may encounter problems around the time you start to think about moving on. If so, I trust that reading this section will encourage you to think things through in more detail, and seek help when needed, in order to find the solution that is right for you.

You will see from the examples below that when you are on your own it can be very difficult to decide what to do for the best. Peter and Maree were doing what seemed right for them, but were finding something was affecting their relationships with others. They just couldn't see the wood for the trees. They were bereaved people who for the first time in years were alone, and had few outside contacts. This meant that they were quite unable to discuss this openly, and understand why, and how they were seen by others. Yet they were in need of outside help if they were to move forward and get on with their life.

Peter

Peter's wife had died more than two years earlier. He lived alone in a very nice house in a pleasant area. Outside and inside it was immaculate. He, or someone, spent a great deal of time keeping it spotless. When you entered the lounge you immediately saw everything was well kept. Furniture looked like new, and appeared to be quite expensive. The room was very crowded. Three settees and an armchair were separated by display cabinets and coffee tables and these were surrounded by dark walls, mahogany shelving and cupboards, all absolutely packed with pottery, glassware, ornaments, photographs and paintings. The only carpet visible was just enough to get you in to somewhere to sit, and out again when you were ready to leave.

Not only did you feel very hemmed in, it was obvious that the room had been arranged by his wife a long time ago. You could feel her strong presence there, and in other rooms downstairs, similarly well stocked. He appeared to have changed nothing, and must have had little time to do anything but keep the house clean and tidy. Sadly, it gave the impression that he had little interest in or time for visitors.

However, he often said that he was lonely, and would have liked more people to come and visit him. In spite of this, he did not hear or act on any suggestions that may perhaps have helped to bring this about. His daughter visited him from time to time, and apparently she supported things remaining exactly the same. So it seems that a lot of water would have to flow under the bridge before his life started to change to meet his new situation, and get him out and about.

Maree

Maree had lost her husband about two years earlier. She was living in local authority accommodation, in a 'single person' dwelling, although she was able to have short-stay visitors from time to time. Her daughter, who had not got on with either of her parents before her father's death, was unemployed and apparently lazy and something of a rebel. She had lived in various places until each time she got told to leave, then moving on somewhere else to repeat the process. About 18 months after her father's death, she decided to join her mother in her home. She managed to move in, and fill the garage with her belongings, before actually asking if she could come and stay. She voiced strong views about her father (which were unwelcome), contributed nothing to household expenses, and spent most of the day in bed.

This obviously held back Maree's recovery from her loss. Maree did not want either to lose her home due to having a long-term visitor staying with her, or to break contact with her daughter. She had loved her husband, but wanted to get on with her life. Eventually she had no choice and took action to make her daughter move out, in order to save her home. She has yet to find out how this has affected her future relationship with her daughter.

Jack

Several years after Jack lost his wife he became friendly with a neighbour, Gillian, who was divorced. They enjoyed a number of outings together. He wanted their friendship to continue, and indeed for it to develop further. However (like Peter above), he was quite unwilling to consider any changes in his home or his habits, in the short or long term. He could not see why his new friend kept suggesting new or different things, or see any need to make changes to his life. Why bother – he already had everything they needed, which was all very nice and had been built up over the years (by his late wife).

Gillian liked Jack very much, and persevered with the friendship, making several attempts to get him to allow her to make some minor changes. Sadly his late wife won, and everything remained the same. Now they are both unhappy, and he still cannot understand why their relationship failed.

A new person entering your life will need to try to understand, and accept, that you are willing to make a fresh start in a new relationship, but that this follows a happy marriage which ended only because of your partner's death. This alone can enable you to see whether a relationship is going to work or not, and possibly set you free to make a fresh choice of companion if you so wish. Likewise, your children, young or grown up, have lost a loved parent. A newcomer has to find a way to create a meaningful and lasting relationship with all of you for the future, as well as fully accept all that has gone on before. However, as you can see, *both* of you need to be willing to make changes, so that it is indeed a fresh start for the two of you.

Remember, all the loving memories are with you for ever, and need not be intrusive. Your situation is quite different from that of someone who has been divorced, and may have been glad to see the other person go out of their life.

Losing your partner through death can give you a better understanding of what is involved in the success of a new relationship. You will certainly be aware of the need for care and caution if feathers are not to be ruffled. Whoever takes up the role has nothing to be jealous about. They are joining you for the next stage of your life. The past has gone before and nothing can change it. The future is there waiting to be filled with happy times, mutual love and respect. But, as you are now well aware, both of you need to be able to make the necessary contribution to achieve this.

A friendly caution

You may meet someone who is very pleasant, makes you happy, and is excellent company – definitely the sort of person you want to get to know better, and spend more time with. This book started with some words of caution, and, sadly, ends in a similar way. There is no rush to begin something new, so take things steadily, and make sure that all newcomers into your life are all they claim to be. If they are genuine they will understand and not be offended.

While I was writing this section, a newspaper reported a court case about a middle-aged woman who had been preying on a number of widowers. She acquired over £100,000 from them in a relatively short space of time. Another report detailed a man building up his wealth by telling hard luck stories. Other stories report that there are people whose aim is to drug, molest or rob those they arrange to meet.

Always remember that a voice on the telephone, or the writer of an email, can be anyone from anywhere. Credentials can be forged or stolen. Therefore, it is essential that you are extremely careful until you are positive that your new companion is genuine. Only give a mobile number yourself – rather than your landline – and never your address until you are sure you want to continue meeting the person in question. You need to know much more about them than a telephone number or an email address.

Never arrange a first meeting in your home or in theirs, or in a lonely place. It is sensible to choose a venue not too far away from where you live, somewhere that you know and feel comfortable about, or that is always crowded, such as a restaurant, pub or garden centre. Arrange your own transport there and back (car or taxi), and do not accept or give lifts to anyone else. Believe in your instincts, and if you are at all unhappy GO HOME. Do not wait and see if things get better.

For the first few meetings, give full details of where you are going to a trusted friend or neighbour. It may seem unnecessary, and a lot of trouble, but it is safer to be cautious, and keep your distance. You have had enough upset and grief in your life recently, and do not need any more. It really is much better to be safe than sorry. Finally, never, *ever*, lend money to anyone. You are meeting only for friendship, not because you provide banking services.

Do not be upset by any of these comments and suggestions. There are still nice, trustworthy people around – it is just that you must be really sure you have found one!

Will there be a happy ending?

The answer to that question must always be 'YES!' – loud and clear.

And hopefully, in many more ways than one. Time is a great healer, and happiness is a state of mind very much in your control. Providing you continue to respond and deal with the challenges of life that come your way, you can and will move forward.

With the help of this book, I hope you will have been able successfully to complete all the work that was facing you: gaining the grant of representation, and carrying out the requirements of the will. If you were able to do everything without any, or much, professional help, then you should be very pleased with yourself. If you felt more comfortable having professional help along the way to bring about a satisfactory conclusion, then so be it, but you should still be happy that it is all behind you.

You may feel that it is worth celebrating – for example, that the strength and confidence you have gained are such that you now feel able to go on holiday. This would probably be very good for you, providing you work up to it, especially if you have led a quiet social life throughout recent months. You need to be very sure of yourself before jumping straight in at the deep end! Tackling such things in easy steps, which build on the new foundations you have created, will ensure happy experiences.

Your partner went on ahead, but would never have wanted you to remain unhappy. You can be sure that he or she would want you to get pleasure from life again by re-entering the world of company, laughter and enjoyment. So, when you have completed all the work, you should find you are able to move along the road to recovery as well.

If you compare your life now with a few months ago, hopefully you will see that you have made a start in finding new friends, especially if you lost some after your bereavement. Also, that your social calendar is starting to take shape, perhaps because you have joined a luncheon group once a month, or taken up a new hobby. Perhaps you attend art classes, or have joined a walking group; some organize walks to see local sights, as well as offering longer, more demanding walks. Lots of social groups, large and small, are waiting for people like you to come and join them.

If you are working, you will have maintained daily contact with other people, and this will no doubt have helped a lot and should make it easier for you to take up new activities to fill up those empty spots in your leisure time. Those who are older and retired but still active may find the voids are on the large side. Take heart – there are still people out there willing to employ you if you look hard enough. The extra money will come in useful too. For those seeking to fill up a few hours, where pay is not important, plenty of charities would welcome you as a volunteer. Helping others in this way can be very rewarding.

Read the local papers and you will find that there are social groups doing all sorts of interesting things – so why not join them? If you continue to smile and move steadily forward, there is a wide range of new and exciting activities and experiences out there waiting for you. When you find your way blocked, treat it as a hurdle, or find a way round it.

The American pioneers seeking a new life encountered rivers, hills and mountains that took them both up and down, and presented them with numerous problems as they moved forward. Their resting place of the moment could be beautiful valleys,

ranches, towns and villages, some nice and others not so nic
kept on going until they found surroundings that suited the....

Now you are in charge of your own wagon train. You can go
as quickly or as slowly as you wish, until you have satisfied your
dreams and heart's desire. You never know, you may meet someone
special. *Good luck!*

Summary – do's and don'ts

A little resume of what we've covered – why not use it as a checklist
while you're taking stock?

Do's

- Do have a healthy diet.
- Do try and keep occupied.
- Do go out and about and keep active.
- Do ensure you get enough rest and sleep.
- Do check your finances regularly.
- Do take extra care to keep your friends.
- Do remember to thank those who help you.
- Do use a new diary and address book.
- Do have a good answerphone.
- Do ensure you remain smart and presentable.
- Do take every opportunity to make new friends.
- Do always carry emergency information on your person when
  out and about.
- Do try and introduce some variety into your life.
- Do give yourself a treat from time to time.
- Do remember to check your will is up to date.
- Do keep your insurances up to date – home, contents, car, etc.
- Do remember to complete a post office mail redirection form if
  you move home.
- Do get your local crime prevention officer to come round and
  check your doors and windows.
- Do attend a few local activities at your village hall or community
  centre.
- Do buy an interesting magazine on a topic you know nothing
  about from time to time.

- Do try and keep up to date with new things – you do not have to actually buy them!
- Do tell friends or neighbours when you do something different, so they know your whereabouts.
- Do have regular medical and dental check-ups.

Don'ts

- Don't take risks.
- Don't tackle dangerous jobs without telling neighbours before and after.
- Don't let strangers into your home.
- Don't forget to treat yourself from time to time.
- Don't become one of the customers with whom banks, building societies and insurance companies lose contact so that your money goes adrift.
- Don't move home without completing a post office mail redirection form for your new address.
- Don't keep a lot of money in your home.
- Don't keep or use any damaged tools or electrical appliances.
- Don't allow carpets to become tripping hazards.
- Don't sit around and mope – your late partner would never have wanted you to be miserable.
- Don't forget to keep your insurances up to date – home, contents, car, etc.
- Don't let you or your home become shabby-looking.
- Don't forget to attend a few local activities at your village hall or community centre.
- Don't forget that there are helplines to solve all sorts of problems – ring up and ask, they are waiting for your call.

Epilogue

The recent months have been an unpleasant time for you. I have tried my best to explain and lead you through it all.

Now the worst time is behind you; do not meekly accept what life puts your way. It really is important that you review your options, move forward, and make a fresh start in the right direction to ensure you begin to enjoy a much happier lifestyle. There is a big difference between 'living', and 'being alive', and you certainly deserve the latter, after all you have gone through recently.

The fact that you have continued to read this book to the very end suggests that it has provided the help and support you needed most, if not all, of the time. I hope so anyway.

As mentioned at the beginning, any comments and suggestions about this book will be welcomed, considered and reviewed. So do get in touch (via Sheldon Press) if you have something to say. This may help in the updating and improving of the contents in later editions, so the book can continue to provide the best possible help and support in the future.

In the meantime, I and my children Suzanne and Nicholas wish you every success in all you do to create and maintain happier surroundings. You will soon realize that it really is worth the extra effort involved.

Appendix 1: Have you got lists?

Some of the following points have been covered in this book – or you may well have thought of them already. However, there's nothing like a list for helping you get organized, especially in the aftermath of this major bereavement, when you are still reeling from the shock.

Personal lists

For administrative matters

- Diary
- Calendar
- A4 ring binders (3)
- A4 loose-leaf lined pads (2)
- A4 lever arch file
- A4 alphabetical division sheet sets (4)
- Address book
- Telephone numbers book
- Cardex file
- A4 writing paper plain pack
- Envelopes to suit above – A4, A5, A6
- Pencils and pens – red/black/blue
- Stapler
- Glue pen/stick
- Rubber
- Sellotape
- String
- Wrapping paper
- Bubble wrap
- Ordinary address labels
- Mini address labels
- Hole punch
- Computer printer items and consumables
- Scanner
- Spare printer ink cartridges – black and colour

- Floppy discs
- Writable/rewritable CDs

For identification purposes

- Current passport
- Current driving licence
- Recent utility bills (in your name)

Transport

- Current bus pass and rail card
- Current bus timetable
- Car tax and MOT renewal dates entered in your diary
- Next car service date in your diary
- Certificate of car insurance, and renewal date in your diary
- Roadside assistance (AA/RAC) membership card in your handbag/wallet, and renewal date in your diary
- Local taxi 24-hour service number on your noticeboard

Health, safety and security matters

Health

- Bathroom scales
- First aid kit and thermometer
- Day/time pill-box
- Small stock of in-date medication (eyewash, paracetamol tablets, cough medicine, etc.)
- Eye test scheduled
- Hearing test scheduled
- Dental appointment scheduled
- Annual health check arranged
- Hospital check-up arranged
- Health/life insurances

Safety

- Mobile phone
- Noticeboard in kitchen or study, with fixing pins
- Torch – with new batteries
- Emergency information in your handbag/wallet and on your noticeboard

- Emergency/useful telephone numbers on your noticeboard
- Talisman SOS pendant or bracelet containing emergency information, to wear
- Saga wrist alarm (tel: 0800 068 5059, <www.saga.co.uk/sos>)
- Spare set of house keys left with a trusted neighbour (and a spare set for you)
- Smoke alarm with new battery
- Carbon monoxide alarm with new battery
- Fire blanket
- Fire extinguisher

Security

- 7 Lever door locks for front and back doors
- Door chains
- Reliable doorbell
- Window locks
- Burglar alarm
- Net curtains or blinds on some downstairs windows, and perhaps upstairs too
- Timers on some room and hall lamps
- Outside security lighting
- Building structure insurance renewal date
- House contents insurance renewal date

For keeping friends and making new ones

- Pocket diary
- Address book
- Birthday book
- Telephone and answerphone, plus BT 1471, 1571
- Mobile phone
- Local newsletter
- Community/village hall activity details
- Library list of local clubs and associations
- Saga membership
- Heyday membership
- U3A membership
- Pack of notelets, envelopes and stamps
- Local papers – some of these are free

- Small collection of greetings cards: thank you, get well, birthday, sympathy
- Stamps, first and second class
- Assorted nice biscuits for visitors

Treats

This list suggests things that might make you feel better, and make your life more enjoyable.

- Flowers
- Digital radio
- Meal out
- New perfume
- New aftershave
- New clothing
- Chocolates
- New hobby
- New activities – keep fit, swimming, evening class, golf
- Part-time work, paid or voluntary
- DVD/CD player
- Bird feeders and bird bath in the garden

Notifications and/or revisions that need to be done

The following list includes some of the organizations that may need to be notified about the death of your partner, in order to cancel existing documents and/or arrangements, and/or transfer some to your name. Some need annual renewal.

It is by no means likely to be a complete list – you might need to add to it, or like to make your own on a separate sheet of paper.

- Annual renewals: car tax and MOT certificate.
- Appointments: cancel dentist, hospital, surgery, etc.
- Associations, professional memberships: revise subscriptions or cancel.
- Banks and building societies accounts, savings, ISA, credit cards, standing orders, direct debits: visit the bank and check what they require, amend joint accounts. Obtain statements regarding all accounts on date of death – these will be needed for probate.

- Book clubs: cancel or revise subscriptions.
- Bus pass: cancel.
- BT: notify, readdress bills in your name.
- Catalogue club accounts (Marshall Ward, Grattan, Empire, etc.): notify, obtain all credits and cancel.
- Central heating boiler: needs annual service.
- Clubs: revise subscriptions or cancel.
- Diary: check if any arrangements need cancelling.
- DVLA: cancel partner's driving licence and update car log book details.
- Electoral register: notify local council.
- Electricity supplier: notify, readdress bills in your name.
- Employer(s): notify.
- Gas supplier: notify, readdress bills in your name.
- Hire purchase agreements: check sum owing.
- Holidays already arranged: cancel or claim on insurance.
- Hospital appointments: cancel.
- House deeds or tenancy agreements: amend names.
- Inland Revenue: notify local office giving National Insurance number.
- Insurance companies, home, contents, car, life and travel policies: check and amend name on policies and other details; claim if appropriate.
- Library: return books, cancel tickets.
- Local authority, council tax: claim reduction if you are now sole occupier plus correct electoral roll records.
- Magazine subscriptions: cancel and claim refunds.
- Medical card: notify and cancel.
- Medical loan items: return equipment (crutches, wheelchair, etc.) to hospital, surgery, Red Cross.
- MOT certificate: check it's up to date/renewal date.
- Motoring breakdown organizations (AA, RAC, Green Flag): revise subscription/cancel.
- National Savings and Investments: notify and close partner's accounts.
- Newspaper deliveries: review needs.
- Passport: cancel partner's.

- Premium bonds: notify, sell partner's holding, perhaps reinvest, check prizes.
- Pension, employer, private, state: advise all of death.
- Professional association: revise subscriptions/cancel.
- Rail card: cancel.
- School(s): notify as needed.
- Security system(s): note when annual service is due.
- Shares: check all holdings, notify and sell. You will need statements of number, values and dividends.
- Social clubs: revise/cancel subscriptions.
- Store cards: notify, cancel and destroy.
- Surgery records, and return of surplus medication: notify and seek guidance.
- Telephone service providers, fixed and mobile: notify and seek guidance.
- TV licence: note when due for renewal.
- Water supplier: notify, readdress bills in your name.
- Your will: update if necessary when it is convenient.

Add any other ones you need below.

_____

_____

_____

_____

Useful social contacts, clubs and activities for you to consider

- Adult classes – day and evening
- Bridge
- Charities
- Church
- Computer club
- Community centre
- Cricket
- Dining out

- Gardening
- Holidays
- Internet
- Library – usually keeps lists of local clubs and societies
- Lions club
- Painting
- Part-time work, paid or voluntary
- Photography
- Probus club
- Rambling
- Rotary club
- Saga
- Swimming
- Tennis
- University of the Third Age (U3A, tel: 020 8466 6139)
- Village hall activities
- Walking
- Wine-making
- Weight Watchers (tel: 08457 123 000)
- Women's Institute

Use the space below to list any you hear about, and have yet to try.

_____

_____

_____

_____

Emergency information

Next of kin
Name:
Tel: Home   Mobile   Work

Neighbour
Name:
Tel: Home   Mobile   Work

Doctor
Name:
Surgery address:
Tel:
Healthcare NHS Trust:

Hospital
Name:
Address:
Tel:
Patient Number:
NHS Number:

Hospital in-patient
Details:
Dates and treatment:

Hospital out-patient
Details:
Dates and treatment:

Current treatment
Details:
Dates and treatment:

Current medication
Details:
Dates and medication:

Dentist
Name:
Address:
Tel:

Solicitor
Name:
Address:
Tel:

Useful telephone numbers

Relatives
Name:
Tel: Home   Mobile   Work
Location:

Name:
Tel: Home   Mobile   Work
Location:

Name:
Tel: Home   Mobile   Work
Location:

Neighbours
Name:
Tel: Home   Mobile   Work
Location:

Name:
Tel: Home   Mobile   Work
Location:

Name:
Tel: Home   Mobile   Work
Location:

Doctor's surgery
Name:
Tel:
Location:
Doctor's name:

Out of hours
Name:
Tel:
Location:

Hospital
Name:
Tel:
Location:

Dentist
Name:
Tel:
Location:

Church
Name:
Tel:
Location:

Minister
Name:
Tel:
Location:

Distant relatives and friends

Name:
Address:
Tel:

Name:
Address:
Tel:

Name:
Address:
Tel:

Solicitor
Name:
Address:
Tel:

Appendix 2: Business letters

When you write to a bank, building society, local authority or other similar large organization, your letter will be one of many received by them that day. Over a year they can expect to receive thousands, perhaps hundreds of thousands, or even millions of communications of one sort or another (think of the number of tax returns, for instance).

To deal efficiently with large volumes of mail, in their communications they will all use a fairly similar format with formal sets of details. Therefore, although you may dislike the formality involved, it is essential that your correspondence conforms to this way of working. The way to get results with minimum problems is to adopt the following guidelines.

Each letter needs to include the following elements.

- Your full address: house name, number, street, town and county, postcode, and full telephone number.
- Today's date (day, month, year).
- Reference details, usually a sequence of numbers and/or letters, supplied by them in recent reply letters, or in the past. The company's 'Our ref' becomes 'Your ref' in your letter; the company's 'Your ref' becomes 'My/Our ref' in your letter.
- The organization's name and address with postcode. Note that replies sometimes come back from another office, so you always need to be able to track any changes.
- 'For the attention of (name and/or title of person, and/or name of department)' (if known, otherwise omit).
- 'Dear (Mr/Mrs/Ms name)' if you know who you are writing to; otherwise 'Dear Sir or Madam'.
- A heading that relates to the contents of your letter. This is likely to include your late partner's full name and date of death. If you are complaining, say so clearly: 'COMPLAINT'.
- The contents of your letter.
- 'Yours sincerely' if you are writing to someone by name; 'Yours faithfully' when 'Dear Sir or Madam' is used.
- Leave a space for your signature.

- Your initials and surname.
- If you need to send a copy of the same letter to someone else, add 'c.c.' followed by the name(s) and department.

If you use a computer, you will find it easy to set out and save a standard layout incorporating the above. Use it as the basis of the first sheet of all your business correspondence. See the typical specimen letters below.

Do not use automatic dating on your correspondence even if you intend to keep a file copy yourself at the time of writing. You must be able to refer back to and at times produce accurate copies of your correspondence. File all your letters in date order.

Useful draft letters

Your full address with postcode
Your full telephone number

Today's date

Your Ref:
My/Our Ref:

Name of organization
Address

For the attention of:

Dear Sir or Madam/Name,

Re: Christian name(s) and surname (deceased) – date of death

Further to my telephone conversation with your helpline staff this morning I shall be grateful if you would provide me with statements for Inheritance Tax/Probate purposes for the following accounts:

Account:
Account:
Premier Account:
(*List types of account, and numbers*)

I understand that each balance needs to include the interest accrued up to and including the date of death, which was (*day, month, year*), and relate to the current tax year.

With thanks,

Yours faithfully,

Initials and surname
Executor (and/or relationship)

Your full address with postcode
Your full telephone number

Today's date

Your Ref:
My/Our Ref:

Name of organization
Address

For the attention of:

Dear Sir or Madam/Name,

Re: Christian name(s) and surname (deceased) – date of death

Further to my telephone conversation with your helpline staff I enclose my wife's/husband's Death Certificate, your latest statement, and my cheque for £___ in full settlement.

I understand that her/his account has been closed, and that you will copy and return the Death Certificate to me. As her/his affairs are subject to Probate I also request that a statement recording this settlement is sent to me, please.

I confirm that all credit cards issued by you to her/him have been destroyed.
Yours faithfully,

Initials and surname
Executor (and/or relationship)

Your full address with postcode
Your full telephone number

Today's date

Your Ref:
My/Our Ref:

Name of organization
Address

For the attention of:

Dear Sir or Madam/Name,

Re: Christian name(s) and surname (deceased) – date of death

I have completed and enclose my Self Assessment form for the last tax year.

My wife/husband died on (*day, month, year*). I called in to (*your town*) tax office to advise them formally, and also notified her/his tax office at (*if different*) while getting advice about how to deal with associated matters.

I trust the enclosed, with the additional information provided, meets your requirements.

Yours faithfully,

Initials and surname
Executor (and/or relationship)

Your full address with postcode
Your full telephone number

Today's date

Your Ref:
My/Our Ref:

Name of organization
Address

For the attention of:

Dear Sir or Madam/Name,

Re: Christian name(s) and surname (deceased) – date of death

My wife/husband died on (*day, month, year*), and I now enclose a Death of a Holder of National Savings form completed on behalf of her/his investments with you, together with the documents listed below.

Copies of the Death Certificate and the Will (please return these documents to me after inspection).

Premium Bonds: (*list of numbers*)

I shall be very grateful if you would provide me with a formal list breaking down the valuations on (*date of death*) for Probate purposes.

I also request that you carry out a trace of the deceased on the full range of your various products, as the details and paperwork I am enclosing may be incomplete.

Yours faithfully,

Initials and surname
Executor (and/or relationship)

Your full address with postcode
Your full telephone number

Today's date

Your Ref:
My/Our Ref:

Name of organization
Address

For the attention of:

Dear Sir or Madam/Name,

Re: Christian name(s) and surname (deceased) – date of death

Further to my telephone conversation with your helpline staff today I am writing to advise you that my wife/husband died on (*day, month, year*), and I am the Executor of her/his will which will be going to Probate.

I enclose a copy of the original Death Certificate for you to copy for your records. Please return this to me.

I have received your valuation advice notes regarding Policy No._____, and shall be grateful if you would also check your records and see if she/he had any other policies with you.

No doubt you will advise me regarding the action you require me to take to progress this matter.

Yours faithfully,

Initials and surname
Executor (and/or relationship)

Your full address with postcode
Your full telephone number

Today's date

Your Ref:
My/Our Ref:

Name of organization
Address

For the attention of:

Dear Sir or Madam/Name,

Re: Christian name(s) and surname (deceased) – date of death

I acknowledge with thanks your letter of (*day, month, year*) and the cheque for £____ following closure of Account No._____. I note that further dividends may follow.

I shall be grateful if you would send me a copy of the associated Certificate of Deduction of Income Tax.

With thanks,

Yours faithfully,

Initials and surname
Executor (and/or relationship)

Your full address with postcode
Your full telephone number

Today's date

Your Ref:
My/Our Ref:

Name of organization
Address

For the attention of:

Dear Sir or Madam/Name

Re: Christian name(s) and surname (deceased) – date of death

Further to our previous correspondence I am now able to proceed with my claim for payment of Policy No._____.

I enclose my completed Bereavement Claim and Direct Transfer Forms, together with a copy of my wife's/husband's Death Certificate and my Grant of Representation. Following inspection, please return both of these to me.

I understand that you will amend Policy No._____ to suit the change in circumstances, and that you will provide me with a final statement as needed for tax purposes.

I believe the above meets your requirements in full, and look forward to hearing from you.

Yours faithfully,

Initials and surname
Executor (and/or relationship)

Useful addresses

Action on Elder Abuse
Astral House
1268 London Road
London SW16 4ER
Helpline: 0808 808 8141
Website: www.elderabuse.org.uk

Age Concern England
Astral House
1268 London Road
London SW16 4ER
Tel.: 020 8765 7200
Helpline: 0800 00 99 66
Website: www.ageconcern.org.uk

Age Concern Northern Ireland
3 Lower Crescent
Belfast BT7 1NR
Tel.: 028 9024 5729
Website: www.ageconcernni.org

Age Concern Scotland
Causewayside House
160 Causewayside
Edinburgh EH9 1PR
Tel.: 0845 833 0200
Website: www.ageconcernscotland.org.uk

Age Concern Wales
Ty John Pathy
13–14 Neptune Court
Vanguard Way
Cardiff CF24 5PJ
Tel.: 029 2043 1555
Website: www.accymru.org.uk

Alzheimer's Society
Devon House
58 St Katharine's Way
London E1W 1JX
Tel.: 020 7423 3500
Website: www.alzheimers.org.uk

Asian Family Counselling Service
Suite 51
Windmill Lane
Southall
Middlesex UB2 4NL
Tel.: 020 8571 3933
Website: www.asianfamilycounselling.org.uk

Asian Funeral Directors
Helpline: 08000 344 6489
Website: www.dignityfunerals.co.uk

Asian Funeral Service
209 Kenton Road
Harrow
Middlesex HA3 0RD
Tel.: 020 8908 3737

Association of Natural Burial Grounds
Website: www.anbg.co.uk
See also **Natural Death Centre**

Bereavement Register
Website: www.the-bereavement-register.org.uk/

Aims to reduce the amount of mail sent to those who have died.

Britannia Shipping Company for Burial at Sea Ltd
Unit 3, The Old Sawmills
Hawkerland Road
Collaton Raleigh
Sidmouth
Devon EX10 0HP
Tel.: 01395 568652

British Association for
Counselling and Psychotherapy
(BACP)
BACP House
15 St John's Business Park
Lutterworth
Leices LE17 4HB
Tel.: 0870 443 5252
Website: www.bacp.co.uk

British Deaf Association Health
and Counselling Service
13 Wilson Patten Street
Warrington
Cheshire WA1 1PG
Tel.: 01925 652 520
Textphone: 01925 652 529

British Humanist Association
1 Gower Street
London SW1V 1PH
Tel.: 020 7079 3580
Website: www.humanism.org.uk

Buddhist Society
58 Eccleston Square
London SW1V 1PH
Tel.: 020 7834 5858
Website: www.thebuddhistsociety.
org

Carers UK
32–36 Loman Street
Southwark
London SE1 0EE
Tel.: 020 7922 8000
Website: www.carersuk.org

Citizens Advice (operating name
of the National Association of
Citizens Advice Bureaux)
Head Office
115–123 Pentonville Road
London N1 9LZ

For local branches, look in your
local phone book.

Community Alarm Services
(Aidcall, Careline, Helplink,
Seniorlink etc.) Small alarms
assisting those living alone.
Obtained via Age Concern above,
and others.

Compassionate Friends
53 North Street
Bristol
BS3 1EN
Tel.: 0117 966 5202
Helpline: 0845 123 2304
Website: www.tcf.org.uk

Contact the Elderly
15 Henrietta Street
London WC2E 8QG
Tel.: 0800 716543
Website: www.contact-the-elderly.
org

Counselling and Psychotherapy
in Scotland (COSCA)
16 Melville Terrace
Stirling FK8 2NE
Tel.: 01786 475 140
Website: www.cosca.org.uk

Cruse Bereavement Care
PO Box 800
Richmond
Surrey TW9 1RG
Helpline: 0844 477 9400
Website: www.
crusebereavementcare.org.uk

Debt Advice Trust
Helpline: 0800 988 7637
Website: www.debtadvicetrust.org

Department for Environment,
Food and Rural Affairs (DEFRA)
Nobel House
17 Smith Square
London SW1P 3JR
Tel.: 08459 556000
Website: www.defra.gov.uk

Dignity in Dying
18 Oxford Street
London W1D 2JT
Tel.: 0870 777 7868
Website: www.dignityindying.org.
uk

Elderly Accommodation Counsel
Third Floor
89 Albert Embankment
London SE1 7TP
Tel.: 020 7820 1343
Website: www.eac.org.uk

Funeral Planning Authority (FPA)
Knellstone House
Udimore
Rye
East Sussex TN31 6AR
Tel.: 0845 601 9619
Website: www.
funeralplanningauthority.com

GayScan
7 Baron Close
Friern Village
London N11 3PS
Tel.: 020 8368 9027
Email: gayscan@blotholm.org.uk

Help the Aged
207–221 Pentonville Road
Tel.: 020 7278 1114
Website: www.helptheaged.org.uk

Heyday
1268 London Road
London SW16 4ER
Tel.: 020 8765 7689
Website: www.heyday.org.uk

For those who are retired or who
are approaching retirement

Holidays
Justyou
Tel.: 0870 252 8008
Website: www.justyou.co.uk

Hospice Information
Hospice House
34–44 Britannia Street
London WC1X 9JG
Tel.: 0870 903 3903
Website: www.hospiceinformation.
info

Human Tissue Authority
Finlaison House
15–17 Furnival Street
London EC4A 1AB
Tel.: 020 7211 3400
Website: www.hta.gov.uk

**Jewish Bereavement Counselling
Service (JBCS)**
Bet Meir
44b Albert Road
London NW4 2SG
Tel.: 020 8457 9710
Website: www.jvisit.org.uk/jbcs

**Law Society of England and
Wales**
Law Society Hall
113 Chancery Lane
London WC2A 1PL
Website: lawsociety.org.uk

Law Society of Northern Ireland
40 Linenhall Street
Belfast BT2 8BA
Tel.: 028 9023 1614
Website: www.lawsoc-ni.org

Law Society of Scotland
26 Drumsheugh Gardens
Edinburgh EH3 7YR
Tel.: 0131 226 7411
Website: www.lawscot.org.uk

Legal Complaints Service
Victoria Court
8 Dormer Place
Leamington Spa
Warwickshire CV32 5AE
Tel.: 0845 608 6565
Website: www.legalcomplaints.org.uk

Complaints about solicitors in England and Wales

London Lesbian and Gay Switchboard
PO Box 7324
Islington
London N1 9QS
Helpline: 020 7837 7324
Website: www.llgs.org.uk

Macmillan Cancer Support (formerly Cancer Relief Macmillan Fund)
89 Albert Embankment
London SE1 7UQ
Helpline: 0808 808 2020
Website: www.macmillan.org.uk

Marie Curie Cancer Care
89 Albert Embankment
London SE1 7TP
Tel.: 020 7599 7777
Website: www.mariecurie.org.uk

Memorials by Artists
Snape Priory
Snape
Saxmundham
Suffolk IP17 1SA
Tel.: 01728 688934
Website: www.memorialsplus.com

National Association of Bereavement Services
Second Floor
4 Pinchin Street
London E1 6DB
Tel.: 020 7709 0505
Helpline: 020 7709 9090 (10 a.m. to 4 p.m., weekdays)

National Association of Funeral Directors (NAFD)
618 Warwick Road
Solihull
West Midlands B91 1AA
Tel.: 0845 230 1343
Website: www.nafd.org.uk

National Association of Memorial Masons
1 Castle Mews
Rugby
Warwickshire CV21 2XL
Website: www.namm.org.uk

National Council for Palliative Care
The Fitzpatrick Building
188–194 York Way
London N7 9AS
Tel.: 020 7697 1520
Website: www.ncpc.org.uk

National Council for Voluntary Organisations
Regent's Wharf
8 All Saints Street
London N1 9RL
Tel.: 020 7713 6161
Website: www.ncvo-vol.org.uk

NHS Organ Donor Register
UK Transplant
Communications Directorate
Fox Den Road
Stoke Gifford
Bristol BS34 8RR
Organ Donor Line: 0845 60 60 400 (24 hours)
Website: www.uktransplant.org.uk

Natural Death Centre
12 Blackstock Mews
Blackstock Road
London N4 2BT
Tel.: 0871 288 2098
Website: www.naturaldeath.org.uk

Probate Service
Contact Court Service/Probate
Registry in your telephone
directory for a booklet on how to
obtain probate.
Website: www.courtservice.gov.uk
Probate and Inheritance Tax
helpline: 0845 302 0900 (Monday
to Friday, 9 a.m. to 5 p.m.)
Website: http://www.direct.gov.
uk/en/RightsAndResponsibilities/
Death/Preparation/
DG_10029716

**Registration of Births, Deaths and
Marriages**
See number in your local phone
book

Relate (National)
Premier House
Carolina Court
Lakeside
Doncaster DN4 5RA
Tel.: 0300 100 1234
Website: www.relate.org.uk

**Relatives and Residents
Association**
Unit 24, The Ivories
6–18 Northampton Street
London N1 2HY
Advice Line: 020 7359 8136 (9.30
a.m. to 4.30 p.m., Monday to
Friday)
Website: www.relres.org.uk

**Royal National Institute for Blind
People (RNIB)**
105 Judd Street
London WC1H 9NE
Helpline: 0845 766 9999
Website: www.rnib.org.uk

Samaritans
PO Box 9090
Stirling
FK8 2SA
National Helpline: 08457 90 90 90
Website: www.samaritans.org

**Society of Allied and
Independent Funeral Directors
(SAIF)**
3 Bullfields
Sawbridgeworth
Hertfordshire CM21 9DB
Tel.: 0845 230 6777
Website: www.saif.org.uk

Terrence Higgins Trust
314–320 Gray's Inn Road
London WC1X 8DP
Tel.: 020 7812 1600
Website: www.tht.org.uk

**UK Parkinson's Disease Society
Tissue Bank**
Division of Neuroscience and
Psychological Medicine
Burlington Danes Building
Imperial College London
160 Du Cane Road
London W12 0NN
Tel.: 020 7594 9732
Website: www.
parkinsonstissuebank.org.uk

United Kingdom Homecare Association Ltd (National)
UKHCA Office
Group House, Second Floor
52 Sutton Court Road
Sutton
Surrey SM1 4SL
Tel.: 020 8288 5291
Website: www.ukhca.co.uk

University of the Third Age
The Third Age Trust
The Old Municipal Buildings
19 East Street
Bromley
Kent BR1 1QE
Tel.: 020 8466 6139
Website: http://www.u3a.org.uk/

Way Foundation
Suite 35, St Loyes House
20 St Loyes Street
Bedford MK40 1ZL
Tel.: 0870 011 3450
Website: www.wayfoundation.org.
uk

Self-help social and support
network for men and women
under the age of 50 who have been
widowed.

What to Do When Someone Dies
Directgov
Website: http://www.direct.gov.uk/
en/Governmentcitizensandrights/
Death/
WhatToDoAfterADeath/
DG_10029808

Which?
Castlemead
Gascoyne Way
Hertford SG14 1SH
Tel.: 01192 822800
Website: www.which.co.uk

Index

activities and hobbies 75–6, 91–2
afterlife and spirit 14–15
Age Concern 19

banks and building societies 89
    dealing with 12, 28–30
    muddles and mistakes 30–1
bereavement
    busy time xiii–xiv
    counselling and aftercare 63–5
    giving away possessions 3
    healing 81–3
    moving on 71–3, 77–80
    need for advice xi–xiii
    recovery from 61–3
    six months on 54–6
    taking stock 66–7

cars 21
Citizens' Advice Bureaux 7, 19
correspondence
    business letters xv, 96–103
    filing 35–6
counselling 64
Cruse 19

death
    identity theft and 5–7
    notifying authorities of 1–2, 8
    reminder list 89–91
death certificates 1, 7, 32
Department for Work and Pensions
    What to do after a death leaflet 18

emotions
    acknowledging 12–14
    changes in relationships 50–4
    living alone xiv
    See also bereavement

family
    funerals and 4
    informing of death 8
    see also friends and neighbours;
        social life

finances
    see money matters
friends and neighbours xv, 69
    changes in relations with 50–4
    finding new friends 75–7
    importance of neighbours 48–50
    informing of death 8
    lists for 88–9
    visiting 70
        see also family; social life
funerals xiv
    burial 18–19
    costs of 17–19
    cremation 18
    making arrangements for 3–5
    pre-payment plans 17–18

health xiv, 87
    recovering from loss 61–3, 67–8
    resting xv
    safety and 59–60
    self-assessment 11
    your diet 68
Help the Aged 19
holidays 69–70
hospices 46
house and home
    DIY and maintenance 43–4
    downsizing 73–5
    gardening 42–3, 45
    housework 38–42, 44–6
    mortgages 21
    personal possessions 78

identity theft xiv, 5–7
inheritance
    see wills
insurance
    dealing with companies 28–30
    first tasks 8
    muddles and mistakes 30–1

legal matters xii–xiii
    dealing with solicitors 26
    documents 9–10

information for 34
    probate requirements 32
    wills and 8
life tasks and skills xiv, xv, 37
    author's experience 44–7
    organizing yourself 34–5
    outside help 37
    personal hygiene 41
    taking stock 68–9
    see also house and home
local council 21–2

money matters xiv
    balances at death 20–1
    dealing with organizations 15–17
    debts 3
    documents 9–10
    frozen funds 12, 21, 29
    identity theft 5–7
    overpayments 12
    record-keeping 22–5
    two months on 31–2

neighbours
    see friends and neighbours

office supplies 86–7
organizations xv, 26–30
    see also banks and building
        societies; taxes

Probate Registry 2, 8
professionals, dealing with 26–8

record-keeping
    dealing with organizations 27–8

documents list 87
    filing 35–6
    finding reliable information 22–5
    first tasks 8
    maintaining 36

Samaritans 19
security and safety xiv, 57–60
    emergency contacts 92–5
    lists for 87–8
    preying people 80–1
social life
    activities and 75–6
    being cautious 80–1
    in bereavement 46–7
    new romance 73, 76–7, 79
support
    changes in friends 50–4
    free advice 19
    hospices 46

taxes xii, xiv
    author's experience 46
    balances at death 20
    dealing with tax office 25–6
    filing information 36
    first tasks 9
    inheritance 3
    record-keeping 25
    tax returns 25, 32
treats 89

utilities 21

wills 2–3, 7–8, 32